SAFEGUARDING STANDARDS

A Report on the Desirability and Feasibility of Establishing a United Kingdom Independent Body to Regulate and Promote Good Practice in Social Work and Social Care

ROY PARKER

Published 1990
by the National Institute for Social Work
5 Tavistock Place, London WC1

© NISW

The text of this publication may not be reproduced in any form without permission from the copyright holders, except for the quotation of brief passages.

ISBN 0902789 68 6

Printed by Icon Impressions Ltd., Yorkshire Street Mill, Bacup, Lancs. OL13 9AF

Steering Group Participants

Robin SeQueira	Director of Social Services, Dorset (Representative of the Association of Directors of Social Services)
David Jones	General Secretary of the British Association of Social Workers
Tony Hall	Director of the Central Council for Education and Training in Social Work
Syd Graham	Deputy Director, Strathclyde Regional Council (Representative of the Association of Directors of Social Work)
Dick Clough	General Secretary of the Social Care Association
Peter Westland	Under Secretary Social Services, Association of Metropolitan Authorities
Stephen Campbell	Under Secretary Social Services, Association of County Councils
Alison Mitchell	NALGO (Representing the TUC)
Colin Thomas	HM Chief Inspector of Probation, Home Office (Observer)
Colin Ralph	Registrar and Chief Executive, UK Central Council for Nursing, Midwifery and Health Visiting
Deirdre Downie	Assistant Secretary of the Convention of Scottish Local Authorities
Bill Utting	Chief Inspector Social Services Inspectorate, Department of Health (Observer)
Malcolm Lacey	Chief Probation Officer, Dorset Probation Service (Representative of the Association of Chief Officers of Probation)
Peter Barclay	President of NISW (Chair)
Daphne Statham	Director of NISW
RESEARCHER	
Professor Roy Parker	Bristol University

Acknowledgements

I have been assisted by many people in preparing this report. They have given their time and shared their views in an exceedingly generous fashion. It would be ludicrous to thank some in particular but I must record my gratitude to the members of the Steering Group, who have given wholehearted support throughout.

The Joseph Rowntree Memorial Trust must also be thanked for providing the financial support without which this report could not have been undertaken.

The views expressed in the report, however, are my own, as are any errors or misunderstandings.

PROFESSOR ROY PARKER
Bristol University

Foreword

Since 1982, when the establishment of an independent body for the regulation and registration of social workers was last considered, there have been many changes in the world of social work and social care. For this reason it was widely felt that the time was ripe for a further and more detailed independent review. Under the auspices of the National Institute for Social Work a Steering Committee was set up in the autumn of 1987. Virtually all the interested bodies were represented on the Committee.

A grant was obtained from the Joseph Rowntree Memorial Trust and we were fortunate in obtaining the services of Professor Roy Parker, whose report is now published.

The matter is still controversial, but in spite of many reasonable arguments which have been advanced against the proposal, Professor Parker has concluded that "the case for a General Social Services Council rather than a Social Work Council has become more compelling since the Barclay Report judged it unproven in 1982".

He believes that in the public interest, and for the reasons he describes, its establishment is now justified.

As we enter a decade of further radical change in the field of social care I hope that this readable, well balanced and authoritative report will be widely read. It should be used as a basis for discussion by those concerned both to improve the standards and quality of social work and personal social services in this country, and also to establish safeguards for the consumer whether in the statutory, voluntary or private sectors.

While the need for discussion is clear, and the interests of those who remain opposed to the proposal must be carefully considered, if we wish to follow the direction in which Professor Parker has pointed, we must not delay the difficult work of negotiation and the planning of appropriate machinery which in due course should lead to the establishment of the Council.

                                    PETER M. BARCLAY
                                    President
                                    National Institute for Social Work

CONTENTS

Part 1 BACKGROUND AND ARGUMENT

1. The Background — 11
2. The Arguments in Favour — 15
3. The Problems and the Objections — 23

Part 2 THE WIDER CONTEXT: CHANGES IN THE 1980s

4. The Composition of the Workforce — 33
5. Inquiries and Public Confidence in Social Work — 41
6. Community Care — 49
7. The Independent Sector — 55
8. National Vocational Qualifications — 61
9. The Reform of Education and Training — 67
10. The European Dimension — 71
11. Social Services Inspection — 75
12. The Local Commissioners for Administration — 81
13. Local Complaints — 87
14. A Review — 93

Part 3 FUNCTIONS, PROCEDURES AND STRUCTURE

15. Registration — 101
16. Discipline — 107
17. Status, Constitution, Structure and Funding — 113
18. Scope — 119

Part 4 THE ESSENTIAL CONCLUSIONS

19. Conclusions — 125

NOTES AND REFERENCES — 127

Part 1

BACKGROUND AND ARGUMENT

This first part of the report briefly sketches the background and history of the idea of a General Council and then sets out the main features of the aguments that have been advanced in its favour and those which have been deployed in opposition.

Chapter 1
THE BACKGROUND

The idea that there should be an independent body for the registration and regulation of social workers goes back at least as far as the early 1950s.[1] However, the fragmented nature of social work activities, combined with a low proportion of qualified staff, weighed heavily against much progress being made. Nevertheless, the idea received a new lease of life in the 1970s, largely as a result of the administrative unification of the local authority personal social services and the opportunity that this provided for the creation of a single professional organisation.

The British Association of Social Workers (BASW) was formed in 1970. One of its objectives was to see a register of social workers established and maintained. However, it did not call immediately for a general and independent body to oversee the accreditation and regulation of social workers and when it did, it encountered some resistance amongst its membership. By the mid-1970s, however, the climate of opinion within BASW had become decidedly more favourable. That may have been the result of the various discussion documents that it had produced in the intervening years; of the changing composition of its membership or of a decline in the social work radicalism that had regarded with suspicion any move which smacked of professional elitism. It was certainly influenced by the public disquiet about the competence of social workers that arose from the publication of inquiries such as that into the death of Maria Colwell.[2]

The proposal for a Social Work Council received overwhelming support in 1976 at BASW's annual general meeting. Steps were taken that led to the establishment of a Joint Steering Group on Accreditation in Social Work. It remained in existence until 1980 when its second and final report was published.[3] The group discussed the nature of accountability and emphasised throughout that the primary purpose of an independent council should be the protection of the public. More specifically, it recommended the creation of a Social Work Council that would be responsible for education and training, accreditation and disciplinary matters. It would include, therefore, the responsibilities of the existing Central Council for Education and Training in Social Work (CCETSW). Alongside the report BASW had prepared a draft Social Work Bill in order to show what kind of legislation would be required in order to set up a General Social Work Council.

Thus, by 1980 a considerable amount of discussion had taken place amongst social workers about the need for such a Council and a blueprint had been prepared. However, the membership of the joint steering group that had done so much to advance the cause of accreditation had been rather narrow. Apart from BASW it had included representatives of the Association of Directors of Social Services; the Residential Care Association (now the Social Care Association); the Conference of Chief Probation Officers (now the Association of Chief Officers of Probation) and, later, the Directors of Social Work in Scotland and the National Association of Probation Officers (although they subsequently withdrew in opposition to the principle of accreditation). Observers attended from CCETSW, the DHSS and the Scottish Social Work Services as well as from the Home Office Probation and After-Care Service. Significantly, though, there were no representatives from the unions, from the local authority associations, or from the voluntary sector. Much of the opposition to the proposal for a General Social Work Council had been expressed by these interests. This was evident once the joint steering group's report was widely circulated and responses invited. In political terms, therefore, the consensus that seemed to have been reached about the desirability of a Social Work Council was of limited applicability.

The Joint Steering Group had been helped in its deliberations by Madelaine Malherbe (formerly social work education adviser at CCETSW). She prepared a series of papers that reviewed the historial context of accreditation in social work; charted developments and drew upon comparative material from other professions and from North America. These papers were published by

CCETSW in 1980.[4] In them Malherbe pointed out that only social work amongst the health and welfare professions in Britain was not subject to the statutory regulation of its training and practice. Nonetheless, she also sounded a number of cautionary notes, indicating 'the limitations of any regulatory system such as registration' and drawing attention to 'the time, effort and expense involved in establishing and maintaining one.'[5] She also concluded that there was little if any evidence from other professions which she examined that accreditation had ensured the protection of the public.

A further opportunity for reviewing the case for a General Social Work Council was provided by the setting up in 1980 of a working party, under the auspices of the National Institute for Social Work (NISW) and chaired by Peter Barclay, to report on the role and tasks of social workers.[6] It received evidence both for and against the establishment of a General Council. BASW in particular urged the creation of such a body whilst the Residential Care Association (RCA) favoured a more broadly-based General Social Services Council. The National Association of Local Government Officers (NALGO) and the National Union of Public Employees (NUPE) opposed the idea as, by and large, did the National Council of Voluntary Organisations (NCVO).[7]

There seem to have been a number of arguments, most of which we shall review later, that carried weight with the working party. However, when it was discovered that social workers themselves were not agreed about the desirability of a Social Work Council the cause appears to have been lost. The report makes the point that only six per cent of the submissions which it received mentioned the matter, and that discussions with social workers around the country provided no evidence that it was regarded as an important issue.

Having reviewed the evidence, and no doubt in light of the divided opinion amongst its members and dubious of the parliamentary support that the proposal could muster, the working party concluded 'that it would be premature' to recommend the establishment of a General Social Work or Social Services Council for the purpose of maintaining standards of practice: that was in 1982. Those who had hoped that the Barclay Report would provide the additional leverage which could put a General Council on the government's agenda were disappointed, whilst those who opposed the idea congratulated the working party on its clear-sightedness.

The British Association of Social Workers in particular continued to press for a Council, as did the Social Care Association (albeit for its particular version); but the failure of the Barclay committee to endorse such a development 'for the moment' effectively put the issue into cold storage for several years. What has caused its reappearance? In order to be able to answer this question it is first necessary to set out the principal arguments that have been advanced in favour of an independent council and then those that have been deployed in opposition. Once this has been done it will be easier to consider which recent changes and developments have a bearing on the strength or weakness of the respective arguments and therefore, perhaps, explain why the proposal for a General Council has re-emerged after the setback it suffered at the hands of the Barclay committee.

Chapter 2

THE ARGUMENTS IN FAVOUR

Stripped of all embellishment, the case for a General Council has rested upon the conviction that since social workers are entrusted with the exercise of considerable discretion they should be subject to mandatory regulation over and above the controls exercised by their employers. Such regulation, it is argued, provides an important measure of protection to those people whose lives are affected by what social workers do. In social work good judgement, compassion and integrity are at a premium, not least because many of those with whom social workers become involved are vulnerable and dependent, in states of crisis or despair. Their predicaments are also apt to present ethical dilemmas.

There are complicating questions about who should or should not be regarded as a social worker, and there are those who query whether social work should be regarded as a profession. These are important definitional problems; but the heart of the case for a General Council appears to lie in what people do rather than in how they are described. Many of those who work in the personal social services are empowered to engage in activities that affect the quality of other people's lives. For that reason they should possess the appropriate knowledge, skill and sensitivity. Whether or not they do is the essential point behind the plea for their regulation in the public interest. The public needs to be assured that those in whom such powers are vested are fit to use them.

However, BASW, for example, has argued that because 'there is no single body which oversees the practice of social work' and because there 'is no control over the use of the title "social worker" . . . the public has no guarantee of any minimum standard of practice from those . . . who claim to be social workers'. Furthermore, it adds, 'there is no accepted national standard against which social work practice may be judged'.[1] It is pointed out that in many professions an established method of dealing with these matters is for a statutory body to be made responsible for maintaining a register and for it to admit to that register only those who are deemed to be competent and who subscribe to an established code of conduct. Furthermore, such a body is also made responsible for removing from the register those who are deemed to be unfit to practise. Such powers enable the public to be protected. Apart from these arguments which BASW presents, it is also the case that certain benefits tend to accrue to those who are registered. They are likely to enjoy a status that is not shared by those who are excluded and they may be more favourably remunerated, although there is not usually an automatic link between salaries and registration.

Of course, as the Merrison committee on the regulation of the medical profession pointed out, such registers are rarely used by the public in any direct fashion.[2] They provide guidance to employers and they can be of value to other agencies that are concerned with the preservation of standards. Nevertheless, the existence of regulative bodies for the professions has provided a means whereby some members of the public have been able to complain about the treatment they have received and, if their complaint was upheld, have disciplinary action taken against the practitioner in question.

If a General Council is empowered to decide who should be placed on its register it follows that it would also have to have the right to specify the requirements for such registration. These, it is maintained, would have to be based upon certain standards of competence. Indeed, the distinction between competence and qualification is an integral part of the case that is advanced for a regulative Council. Although CCETSW has the authority to approve courses, the assessment of students' performance remains mainly the responsibility of educational institutions (with all the opportunities for variation that that offers, despite the use of external examiners). Individual practice thereafter may or may not reflect qualifications and, in any case, it may become increasingly unrelated to them (for better or worse) as time passes. Moreover, competence is built on experience as well as qualification. It would be necessary therefore for that competence to be assessed. Only after it had been established that someone was competent would they be registered.

However, if a General Council is to specify the conditions for registration then it will have to exercise a substantial measure of influence over the nature of education and training as well as over the determination of competence. That being so, all the advocates of a regulative Council agree it would have to incorporate the present functions of CCETSW, and indeed these would probably have to be extended. Were this to happen, it is argued, it would bring a greater degree of coherence to the hotch-potch of qualifications, assessments of competence and regulation that currently defeat the establishment of national standards.

Alongside the logical and necessary link with education and training, a council would have to formulate or adopt a general code of conduct by which those whom it registered were bound. Beyond that, however, there is a range of specific areas where codes of conduct and guidelines for practice are required. At the moment such publications are issued by an assortment of organisations. There are, for example, those drawn up by BASW for its members, especially its Code of Ethics, and the Code of Practice for Social Care prepared by the SCA.[3] An increasing number of guidelines are also issued by the Department of Health. Some local authorities and independent organisations have compiled similar documents. However, these standard-setting prescriptions do not cover all social workers and social care staff and they differ in their emphasis as well as in the sanctions that are available, should the practitioners to whom they apply fall short of what is expected. A General Council could draw up a definitive code of conduct that would bind all those whom it registered. Not only would there be a greater uniformity in the determination of competence, therefore, but also a common definition of good conduct.

As well as the value of its fulfilling functions such as these, it is maintained that there are other public benefits that would follow from the establishment of a General Council. There is, for example, the likelihood that other professions, most notably medicine, would be more willing to collaborate (especially in the exchange of sensitive information) with those whom they knew to be registered practitioners trained to a certain level and subject to a professional code of conduct.

However, it would be foolish to believe that registration alone will resolve deep-seated problems of collaboration. Nevertheless, anything that serves to improve mutual confidence and trust is to be welcomed, given that the quality of service that people receive so often depends upon successful inter-disciplinary co-operation.

The need for a means of setting national standards is accentuated, it is claimed, because employers who might be expected to monitor the competence of their employees either do not do so, or apply a variety of standards. The Association of Directors of Social Services has levelled that criticism with some force. There is concern, they say, about

> the variable response of employing agencies to perceived or proven incompetence. The not infrequent introduction of political perspectives and responses, be they subtle or obvious, into the arena of judgement of competence (and subsequent disciplinary sanctions) has done little to promote the confidence of the public and professionals in the current ability of those very employers to remedy faults.

That, they argue, suggests that an independent regulative body is required that is 'unshackled by politics or purely local considerations'.[4] As a result, not only would the public be better safeguarded but practitioners would be protected against the vagaries of local systems: they too would know better where they stood.

Indeed, the question of public confidence is a prominent feature of the case made for a General Council by both BASW and ADSS. BASW has pointed out that the effective operation of the personal social services depends upon a measure of public confidence in social work. That confidence, it considers, is being eroded; not least by hostile media. If it is to be restored and enhanced steps have to be taken to show that social work is putting its house in order, and that allegations about incompetence can be dealt with in an independent fashion and by the application of agreed national criteria. The ADSS also stresses that 'there is currently no effective counter to those who highlight the absence of a standardised system of assessment of competence of professionals charged with high risk cases or indeed tasks of lower status and danger'.[5]

Thus, a variety of arguments has been deployed in favour of a General Council; but those that we have considered so far largely derive from what might be termed the social work tradition. Indeed, many of the papers refer specifically to a General *Social Work* Council, although there is a continuing debate about the range of activities that the term social work should cover. For example, some see social care as part of social work and others view social work as a component of social care. Terminology (and the attitudes that it reflects) is in a state of flux. Thus, the arguments for a General *Social Services* Council have many things in common with those that are deployed in favour of a Social Work Council; but they also reflect a different emphasis.

The SCA has argued for a system of registration that is as inclusive as possible in order to cover 'all individuals who are in positions of power over clients, whether physically or because of their authority and status'. This would include unqualified (or unaccredited) staff in positions of responsibility. Only in this way, the SCA points out, will it be possible to extend the safeguards that registration and de-registration offer to the great majority of those who use the personal social services, including both the voluntary and the private sectors. The criteria for registration could be modified over time as training became more extensive.

However, the SCA has conceived a General Council that not only administers a broadly-based system of registration, regulation and standard-setting but which performs other functions in addition. The inclusion of these extended functions (some of which are advocated by other bodies as well) is considered to strengthen the case for an independent body. Three suggestions in particular are notable.

First, there is the call for a General Council to be the standard-bearer for the personal social services or, depending upon the emphasis, for social work. At last, there would be a single body that offered 'coherent leadership' and was able to speak 'with a more united voice'.[6] It could be, in the words of one BASW note, 'a powerhouse for the development and promotion of professional social work' and would be a force to ensure that attention was paid to 'the qualitative aspects . . . of practice'.[7] In these senses a Council would act as a major advocate, interpreter and defender in matters that affected the quality of the services, thereby helping to ensure that users had a better deal. Some consider this to be the strongest part of the case for a General Council.

Secondly, there is the idea that a Council could or should have the power to conduct inquiries into *prima facie* failures of a service to protect or assist those for whom it has or should have a responsibility. These would be inquiries into specific cases along lines recommended by the Blom-Cooper report on the death of Kimberley Carlile.[8] The Council might appoint a standing committee for such purposes, or at least nominate a permanent chairperson. Such a committee would be available to the minister, to local authorities or other organisations. It would have no power to act uninvited. Nonetheless, it would avoid the need for a new committee of inquiry to be convened afresh on each occasion. This would enable a body of experience to be built up and shared (perhaps through an annual report). Furthermore, it could be related to any hearing of allegations of misconduct against the individual social workers or social care staff involved and, some would argue, thereby ensure that their case would be examined against all the relevant circumstances. In short, as the SCA suggests, 'a national body could be used to provide a more standardised system of independent inquiry' into a field that has been subject to many types of inquiries following different procedures and reporting to different authorities.

The third theme that is elaborated in support of a General Council assuming extended responsibilities (and which, it is contended, thereby strengthens the case) concerns research. It would be impossible for a Council to operate properly unless it possessed key information (for example, about the size and composition of the workforce). It would have to take steps to ensure that such data were available and conveniently assembled. This would be of general importance and contribute to workforce planning, especially to its training aspects. Obviously, CCETSW generates and collects some of this information already: the contention is that under a General Council with a wider responsibility these processes would be improved and elaborated.

However, there is a stronger version of this argument; namely, that a General Council should undertake, commission or orchestrate research of a much more general kind that was relevant to service standards.

These further arguments raise important issues that would need to be addressed in formulating the responsibilities of any Council. However, if they are divorced from questions of registration, regulation and standard-setting, they become part of a case for a rather different independent body than this review was invited to consider.

Chapter 3

THE PROBLEMS AND THE OBJECTIONS

One of the principal objections to the creation of a Council that administers a register of those who are considered to be competent to practise springs from the necessarily selective nature of that process. There is an assortment of staff working in the personal social services who, although they carry considerable responsibility for dealing with taxing and stressful situations, are unqualified. In particular, fewer social care staff have a formal qualification than field social workers. If, on that ground, many of them were to be excluded from registration then, it is feared, they would be discredited and the value of their contribution diminished. Public confidence in them and the work that they do would be undermined. It would be that much more difficult to improve the sad state of their present remuneration. On all these counts morale would be likely to suffer and with it the possibility of maintaining or raising standards, especially in residential care.

This view has been propounded by the unions involved (NALGO and NUPE) and also by the Social Care Association. However, as we have seen, the SCA has lent its enthusiastic support to the idea of a more broadly conceived General Council that registers a wide range of staff, both qualified and unqualified. They would still wish to apply certain conditions to registration but would define them in ways that did not automatically exclude some 80 per cent of social care staff and therefore a large proportion of all practitioner staff in the personal social services.[1]

If the standing of social care is indeed depressed by the exclusion of most of its staff from a system of registration, then those who rely upon that care will be adversely affected. The objection to a Council on these grounds has to be taken especially seriously.

There is the additional argument (for example developed by NALGO in its evidence to the Barclay committee) that should registration be open to a wide cross-section of staff, it would defeat its primary purpose of protecting the public because so many of those already practising would have to be blanketed-in without having had to satisfy any requirement as to qualifications, or having had their competence established in some other way. NALGO has linked this argument with the view that the task of actually identifying staff who would be eligible for registration is beset by practical difficulties, not least those associated with what it contends is the absence of a recognised core of knowledge in social work, and therefore of a basis for formulating good practice and conduct.[2]

A somewhat different objection was noted by the Barclay committee amongst its reasons for not recommending the establishment of a General Council: namely that the existence of registration would enhance the status of the profession at the expense of the closer involvement of clients. Furthermore, it would weaken the confidence of community groups to engage in local action and self-help. For example, the evidence of the National Council of Voluntary Organisations maintained that 'the primary skill of a social worker should be to unlock the resources in the community', but that further steps towards the professionalisation of social work would impede change in that direction.[3] In essence this, and similar arguments, rest upon the view that registration will foster professional elitism to the detriment of good social work and social care, because it thereby creates a gulf between certain helpers and the helped that then institutionalises dependence.

Another major objection to the establishment of a General Council with disciplinary powers is raised by the employer interests as well as the unions, but especially by the Association of Metropolitan Authorities (AMA). They considered that disciplinary responsibilities must reside with the employers with whom staff are in a contractual relationship. In their view a General Council that superimposed another system of discipline would not only be a duplication, but would usurp functions that are and should continue to be exercised by employers. The existing framework of industrial relations would be seriously disrupted.

Such concern is raised in these terms because most social services staff are employed by local government. However, the general issue of separating the two domains has had to be faced in the case of other professions such as law, where solicitors are employed by local authorities. Similarly, in the case of medicine and nursing a distinction has been drawn between practitioners' accountability to their employers for fulfilling the terms of their contract, and their accountability to their profession for their professional conduct; that is, for their observation of its code or codes of ethics and conduct. Thus, the General Medical Council's (GMC) function is 'limited to cases where doctors are convicted of criminal offences or misbehave in a manner amounting to serious professional misconduct'.[4] Less serious misdemeanours or allegations of incompetence are dealt with by the disciplinary procedures that exist within the National Health Service (NHS). This demarcation appears to provide a basis for distinguishing between the jursidiction of a regulative body for the profession and the employers.

In fact, however, matters are by no means so clear-cut, as the recent report of the GMC's working party on disciplinary procedures makes plain.[5] They were asked to consider whether the Council's existing system afforded 'an appropriate means of determining alleged failures by doctors in the standard of care provided in individual cases, where the underlying issue appears to be one of failure of competence rather than serious professional misconduct'. In the case of medicine the heart of the matter is the relationship between serious professional misconduct and serious professional incompetence. The presumption has been that these could be treated as separate categories, and therefore that the disciplinary jurisdictions of the profession and the employers could also be disentangled. In the event, the GMC's working party recommended that further consideration should be given to the matter, especially in light of the impending introduction into the NHS of arrangements whereby consultants and general practitioners would be placed under a contractual obligation to take part in medical audit — that is, the scrutiny of their practice. However, as the government's white paper on the NHS points out, although 'medical audit will be contractually required it is essentially a professional matter' to be conducted through processes of peer and self-review.[6]

Nonetheless, professional audit leaves the issue of disciplinary jurisdiction unresolved. Its continuing complexity is indicated by a judgement of the Judicial Committee of the Privy Council (in the case of a dentist), which found that 'serious professional misconduct may include very serious errors in treatment which fall considerably short of expected standards'.[7] Serious professional incompetence therefore could be considered to be serious professional misconduct. In 1984 the GMC broadened its guidance about the scope of its disciplinary proceedings to include cases that arose from allegations of 'failure to provide a proper standard of care'. This included, for example, the failure of a doctor to provide 'competent and considerate professional management'.[8] There is obviously an overlap between professional incompetence and professional misconduct, not least in terms of a practitioner's failure to accept opportunities for improving or bringing up-to-date his knowledge or skill. As well as this there are the situations where incompetence is attributable to illness, alcoholism or drug addiction.

It is clear that most allegations of professional incompetence, and even of professional conduct falling short of expected standards, should be dealt with at the local level; and that means by employers. However, there are some difficulties in adopting this prescription over and above the problem of settling jurisdictions. Three in particular may be noted. First, unlike medicine and nursing, there is no major single employer in the personal social services and although there is a nationally recommended code of disciplinary practice and procedures drawn up by the Advisory, Conciliation and Arbitration Service (ACAS), it is couched in general terms that allow for considerable local variation.[9] Moreover, there is nothing comparable with the formal NHS 'list' that ensures that staff who have been dismissed for incompetence or misconduct can also be removed from, as it were, an employers' register. Someone dismissed by a local authority for serious shortcomings could be re-engaged elsewhere by an employer unaware of the background. Secondly, there is the problem of discipline in the private or voluntary sectors where, although the ACAS code of practice remains the recommended guideline, an ever greater variety of disciplinary practices (or none at all) prevail. Thirdly, there is the question of public and employee confidence in employer systems of discipline. Some feel that these are not always applied as scrupulously as they should be, and thus introduce further crucial variations between one area and another.

Alongside concern about the conflict of jurisdictions there is the fear that the existence of an independent Council, with its own disciplinary powers, will create a situation in which practitioners are placed in double jeopardy. This possibility cannot be denied, but it would be no different from what prevails in certain other professions. For instance, doctors are liable to have to answer to some ten different statutorily-based disciplinary systems. However, if practitioners are to be subject to more than one procedure it is crucial that it is clear in which circumstances each is invoked, and that they do in fact deal with different matters or a different implication of the same matter. Even achieving that, however, leaves unresolved a problem raised by NALGO; namely, that a situation could arise where a General Council took disciplinary action against an individual social worker independently of the employer and perhaps against their wishes. This, the union points out, 'would be absolutely alien to the industrial relations framework within which local authorities operate'.[10] Whether that would affect the public interest is another matter.

There is a different and more widely expressed anxiety, that any registration and disciplinary system that deals with individual practitioners will allow (however unwittingly) corporate bodies to escape criticism and disavow their responsibilities. In short, there is the fear that individuals will be made scapegoats for deficiencies that lie quite outside their control. This potential danger has been recognised by bodies such as the United Kingdom Central Council for Nursing, Midwifery and Health Visiting (UKCC). It recently reiterated its disquiet about 'the continued misuse and abuse of enrolled nurses, many of whom are expected to perform a role for which their training did not and was not expected to prepare them, only to become the subject of complaints when not quite satisfying these expectations'. The UKCC were also concerned about 'the frequency with which practitioners appearing as respondents before the Committee (especially from the less fashionable specialties) are people who have been employed in settings which are seriously understaffed or inappropriately staffed to the point at which both patient and practitioner are endangered'.[11] It is clear that some allegations have been made against nurses for incompetence when that 'incompetence' has been largely the result of their having to work in situations that did not permit competent and responsible work to be done. In dealing with such allegations, the UKCC has been at pains to protect nurses from unfair criticism and therefore has provided an important safeguard against scapegoating.

There are, of course, two dimensions in the scapegoating issue. One is the potential unfairness of submitting practitioners to disciplinary proceedings in circumstances where they have been more sinned against than sinning, and the other is the opportunity that this offers for attention to be deflected from the structural or political factors that may have precipitated the breakdown in the standard of service provided. The first matter could be dealt with by the way in which the scope of a Council's disciplinary jurisdiction was defined and its procedures designed. The danger of the second consequence, which NALGO characterises as the risk of 'diversion' can, it argues, only be reduced by the existence of other effective means by which structural deficiencies can be identified and effective pressure mounted for them to be made good.

However, some bodies such as BASW point out that the existence of a General Council with disciplinary power could well protect staff from being scapegoated at the local level. At present, for example, when a social worker is disciplined the only tribunal, apart from formal appeals, is presided over by the employer. If there is a failure of service due to structural shortcomings it may be in the employer's interest to allow the blame to fall on the individual. The danger of scapegoating and unfairness may well be greater under these circumstances than it would be in a system operated by an independent national Council which could offer a more disinterested hearing, as well as highlighting any organisational or resource deficiencies.

As well as the objections that arise from the proposed disciplinary powers of a General Council, there are others that are based upon broader and more general misgivings. It is argued, for example, that if the need for a Council is judged against its likely contribution to the improvement of standards, then the case falls because it fails to address certain crucial problems. These are seen to be issues such as the reform and expansion of training; the provision of additional resources; the development of preventive strategies; the enlargement of knowledge and understanding; the improvement of management or the greater participation of users in determining the nature and pattern of services. A General Council, it is charged, can do little to realise these goals and is, therefore, largely irrelevant to the main issues of the day.

Something of this sentiment was captured in the report of the Barclay committee, where it was concluded that an independent Council was not the most appropriate means of raising standards and protecting the public. Other ways forward were preferred: for instance, the introduction of a probationary period for newly-qualified social workers; the monitoring of social work practice and of the performance of their employing agencies by an independent inspectorate; the formalisation of the rights of clients together with clear means of complaint or appeal and, finally, the establishment of local welfare advisory committees to provide a consumer viewpoint on the development of policy.[12] However, not all of these 'alternatives' have been implemented.

While it has to be admitted that a General Council neither should nor could be expected to perform some of these functions, it is relevant to consider whether the case for its establishment is strengthened by the development of other means of improving standards and protecting the public, or whether it is weakened or untouched. One important factor that affects the answer is the extent to which a General Council would incorporate, or be closely allied to, CCETSW. It there is an integration then it could certainly be expected to exercise a good deal of influence over education and training through its power to determine the conditions of registration. That apart, however, it must be granted that what a regulative Council could do to alter other powerful determinants of the standard of services would be limited, although not necessarily negligible. Even so, it would be unreasonable to expect it, or any other single institution for that matter, to exercise conclusive influence. The politics of social policy are more complicated than that.

Thus the objections to a General Council derive from two principal sources. One concerns the question of who is and who is not to be registered, and the other is the scope of its disciplinary jurisdiction and the procedures through which that would be fulfilled. If the objections to either registration or discipline (or both) are sustained then the case for a General Council is in peril. That is not to say that a body charged with some of the other responsibilities that it has suggested a Council should accept (such as reaserch or the formulation of codes of conduct or practice) would be unnecessary; simply that the debate about such a body, its composition and functions, should be conducted in a different manner (and probably by different interests) than that about the need for a regulative Council.

Part 2

THE WIDER CONTEXT: CHANGES IN THE 1980s

This second part reviews the main changes that have occurred in the wider context in which a consideration of the need for a General Council has to be set. In particular it concentrates on changes that have arisen since the publication of the Barclay Report.

Chapter 4

THE COMPOSITION OF THE WORKFORCE

As we have seen, one of the persistent objections to any system of accreditation and registration of social workers has been (and continues to be) that it would be likely to exclude large numbers of existing personal social services staff who are unqualified or considered to be insufficiently qualified. Were that to happen, it is argued, it would accentuate and perpetuate the divisions that lead to the devaluation of the contribution of those who are not formally qualified. Furthermore, it has been maintained, whilst registration remained selective it would do comparatively little to protect the interests of clients, most of whom would continue to be dealt with by staff who were excluded from the system.

These are persuasive arguments and, looking back over the post-war history of the personal social services it is plain that, unlike other professions, social work has continued to employ many unqualified staff, at least in the sense of their not having passed a relevant qualifying examination. For example, the Younghusband Report on social workers in the local authority health and welfare services conducted an inquiry into the pattern of staffing and found that in 1956 only eight per cent of field staff possessed some kind of social science qualification, although one in five of them held a poor law relieving officer's certificate or its Scottish equivalent.[1] The survey failed to obtain any reliable information about residential staff. In children's departments (which Younghusband did not look into) the proportion of qualified staff was higher, although no systematic collection of data was undertaken until 1964, and only then for field workers. In that year about 27 per cent of the staff of English and Welsh children's departments were recognised as qualified by the Home Office.[2]

In 1967 the Seebohm committee estimated that of the 10,000 or so social workers in England and Wales 43 per cent had a professional qualification.[3] However, this proportion was boosted by a high level of qualified staff in the probation service; if they were excluded the proportion fell to 35 per cent.[4] Once again, however, no reliable data were available about residential care staff; nor was there information about the voluntary or private sectors.

The first reasonably complete survey of 'manpower and training' in Great Britain was undertaken by the Birch committee which reported in 1976.[5] A rapid increase in all categories of staff had accompanied the re-organisation of the personal social services following the recommendations of the Seebohm committee; for example, between 1972 and 1974 there had been a 25 per cent increase. By then, the Report estimated, the proportion of qualified field staff in local authorities stood at 35 per cent and at eight per cent for residential care staff. However, as pointed out by CCETSW, a further 23 per cent of the 8,500 residential care staff for whom information was available had undergone some relevant training.[6] Nevertheless, that still left two-thirds of them without any form of qualification or training.

With the assistance of CCETSW and the Local Government Training Board (LGTB) the Barclay committee also assembled information about social work staffing in England and Wales.[7] It was calculated that in 1980 there were some 15,700 field social workers, a further 5,000 team leaders and 4,000 in management or advisory posts. Over 70 per cent of those employed in 'front line' social work were qualified. For those in management positions the proportions rose to 90 per cent. Some 60 per cent of social workers in the voluntary sector were estimated to be qualified. However, of the 28,000 residential care staff employed by local authority departments there were still only 15 per cent who possessed a social work or social services qualification. A slightly higher rate of qualification (17 per cent) was found amongst residential care staff employed by voluntary agencies.

Thus, the estimated proportion of qualified staff, both in social work and social care, had doubled in the six years between 1974 and 1980. This was mainly attributable to the expansion of training, especially to the introduction of the Certificate in Social Service in 1976 but also to a 33 per cent growth in the output of courses for which the Certificate of Qualification in Social Work (CQSW) was awarded. These increases were somewhat offset by a reduction in the number of students qualifying for residential work. Nevertheless, the overall trend was upwards.[8]

Obviously the expansion of training was not the only factor at work in doubling the proportion of qualified staff in local authority social services departments in the period between the Birch Report and that of Barclay. There was also a slowing down in the rates of wastage as well as the beginning of the expansion of part-time employment, which may have been associated with the return to employment of older trained staff.

Whatever the precise reasons there was, by 1980, an undeniably larger proportion of qualified staff being employed in local authority social services departments than there had been at the beginning of the 1970s. Nonetheless, it still left a sizeable minority of unqualified field social workers and a large majority of unqualified residential care staff. These facts continued to lend support to those who held the view that any system of registration which was based upon qualification would be divisive and leave many clients unprotected because of its partial coverage.

In 1986 the Local Government Training Board conducted a survey into manpower and training in the personal social services on behalf of the Association of County Councils (ACC), the Association of Metropolitan Authorities (AMA) and the Convention of Scottish Local Authorities (COSLA).[9] It found that 85 per cent of the 25,000 field social workers in Great Britain possessed a social work qualification. The proportions were highest in Scotland (97 per cent) and lowest in the Welsh counties (77 per cent). The overall rate represented a substantial increase from the 70 per cent estimate that was available to the Barclay working party. This was an important change, for it brought nearer to the point of 'critical mass' the proportion of qualified social workers that would be necessary to be able to proceed to a fully registered profession without encountering the difficulties that would arise were such a move to be made with much lower levels of qualified staff. Moreover, by the time that any system of registration could be introduced it would be reasonable to assume that the rate of qualification in field social work would be even higher.

However, the position amongst other social services staff remained both complicated and problematic. For instance, the conclusion drawn from the LGTB's 1986 survey about the extent of qualifications amongst the staff of residential and day care services for children was as follows:

> If professional social work qualifications only are considered, 11.5 per cent of staff are qualified. However, this figure is distorted by nurseries and family centres, which have the lowest level of social work qualified staff (3.5 per cent) but the highest level of appropriately qualified staff overall. If nurseries and family centres are taken out of the figures entirely, the overall percentage of staff with a relevant social work qualification rises to 14.5 per cent.[10]

There was, however, a wide variation around this overall rate of qualification according to the type of establishment; for instance, it stood at nine per cent in homes for mentally and physically handicapped children but was 50 per cent in intermediate treatment centres.

Turning to residential and day care services for adults, the LGTB report showed that:

> Overall 7.5 per cent of staff hold a social work qualification and 24 per cent . . . hold either a social work qualfication or another relevant qualification such as one of the nursing or teaching qualifications, or the Diploma in Teaching the Mentally Handicapped.[11]

The highest levels of social work qualification were found amongst staff working with the mentally ill (14 per cent), and the lowest (leaving aside a small number of miscellaneous homes and centres) amongst those working with the elderly (7.5 per cent).

The third category of staff (some 5,000) identified by the LGTB survey were those classified as working in domiciliary services. However, there are difficulties arising from this classification because half the authorities that responded to the survey had integrated their domiciliary services with field work teams. Most of those who were specified as domiciliary care staff were in fact managers of one kind or another. Nonetheless, the list of the types of other staff indicated a wide variety of tasks; for instance family aides, home care assistants and wardens of sheltered housing. Overall, whereas amongst the managers of domiciliary services the rate of qualification in social work was 18.5 per cent, it was only 5.5 per cent amongst all other posts in this field.[12]

The conclusion to be drawn from the LGTB survey data about residential, day care and domiciliary care staff must be that the situation described by the Barclay Report, and by the Birch inquiry earlier, had remained (at least until 1986) substantially unchanged. The problem of the widely different extent of qualification as between field work staff on the one hand and care staff on the other was as pronounced as ever. Indeed, since the LGTB study did not include workers in manual grades, many of whom work with dependent people in residential and day care settings, the situation may actually have deteriorated.

However, these are conclusions about what has been happening in the local authority social services. Little is known about the situation in the voluntary or private sectors. The Birch Report concluded that information about voluntary organisations was 'not sufficiently complete to be reproduced' and made no comment at all about staff working in private agencies.[13] The Webb committee that reported on workforce planning and training need in 1987 did make some estimates but admitted that they had been obliged 'to cloak their ignorance in plausible assumptions'. The only figure that they were able to offer for the voluntary sector related to managerial staff, 40 per cent of whom were thought to hold a social work qualification.[14] My enquiries of the major voluntary child care organisations suggest that 60 to 70 per cent of their social work staff are qualified. Information on the private sector is even more sparse and, like the Birch committee before it, the Webb committee hazarded no guess about the proportion of staff who were qualified although, of course, the private residential care sector has expanded dramatically in the last ten years.

The most up-to-date workforce information comes from a survey of social services employment in England and Wales conducted by the Local Authorities Conditions of Service Advisory Board (LACSAB) and the ADSS in November, 1988. It did not include the private or the voluntary sectors. Nonetheless, its results are of considerable importance. First, it found that 87.5 per cent of full-time field social workers were professionally qualified (defined in accordance with the NJC Scheme and Conditions of Service). This excluded team leaders amongst whom one might have expected a higher rate (the LGBT survey found 90 per cent amongst senior social workers). Of the part-time field social workers 88.6 per cent were qualified. Rates of qualification were higher amongst men than women; for example 90 per cent as compared with 86 per cent amongst the full-time staff and 98 per cent and 88 per cent respectively amongst the part-timers.

Thus, overall, 88 per cent of field social workers in post at the end of 1988 were qualified and if senior staff are added the figure almost certainly exceeds 90 per cent. However, it is significant that nearly half of the full-time qualified social work staff obtained their qualification between 1984 and 1988. That does not necessarily imply a young workforce, for almost half of them had qualified at 30 or over and there was a significant proportion who were over 40. As the report suggests, this points to a rather mature workforce.[15]

It needs to be borne in mind that all the figures that have been reviewed apply to staff in post. The LACSAB-ADSS survey had the additional merit of looking at vacancy rates in some detail. For full-time field social workers the overall figure was 10.6 per cent and for part-timers 8.8 per cent.[16] There were, however, considerable differences between regions and between local authorities. Greater London had the highest rate (16.4 per cent) and the Southern region the lowest (4.7 per cent). The differences between the individual local authorities (71 per cent of whom made a return) were dramatic. A few had no vacancies for field social workers, whilst in London there were departments with 43 per cent (the highest), 37 per cent, 30 per cent and 26 per cent of their posts unfilled; and some of the London boroughs known to be facing the most severe problems of recruitment were amongst those that did not provide information. Outside London the highest vacancy rates fell between 15 and 20 per cent.[17]

Vacancy rates (though fraught with difficulties of comparability) have a bearing upon the interpretation of qualification rates, on recruitment and training policies and, of course, they affect the level of pressure under which staff are obliged to work.[18] That may well affect the likelihood of allegations being made about incompetence which, given the circumstances, are unfair. The implications of registration by a General Council, and particularly its disciplinary powers, could thus be differently experienced in different areas.

Finally, it must be added yet again that important though it was, this survey did not include residential or day care staff. We remain as uninformed about them as we were before, although it is suggested that this deficiency might be rectified by a future LACSAB-ADSS joint venture.

However, these and other data indicate that important changes in the proportion of field staff who are qualified have occurred since the Barclay committee reported in 1982. There has been the continuing movement towards the employment of only qualified social workers in local authorities. In Scotland the process is virtually complete, while in probation nobody who has not been awarded a Certificate of Qualification in Social Work (or an approved equivalent) is permitted to be appointed as a probation officer or any more senior rank.[19]

There is little doubt that in general (it may be different in a number of particularly hard-pressed authorities) we have reached a stage where a system of registration based upon qualifications and the subsequent assessment of competence could be introduced for field social workers without it precipitating the difficulties that would have arisen in doing so when rates of qualification were at much lower levels. In sharp contrast residential, domiciliary and day care staff remain largely unqualified, but not necessarily untrained, inexperienced or incompetent. If their registration were to be linked to qualification then most of them would be excluded with the undesirable consequences, such as a further devaluation of their work, that that would entail.

Chapter 5

INQUIRIES AND PUBLIC CONFIDENCE IN SOCIAL WORK

We have already seen that the deterioration of public confidence in social work is one of the factors adduced in favour of the argument for a regulative General Council. It is maintained that the imposition of clear national standards, as well as the creation of a means by which social workers could be held accountable for their actions, would help to restore that confidence. How much loss of confidence there has been is open to debate; in any case it is greatly influenced by media reporting. The performance of the personal social services and their staff become particularly newsworthy when something goes seriously wrong. Case tragedies and scandals attract attention. Many such sad events have been investigated by committees of inquiry, whose findings provide elaborate evidence indicating that all is not well. Many of the most widely reported cases have concerned the death or abuse of children for whom social services department had, or were assumed to have had, responsibility.

Between the Monckton inquiry into the death of Dennis O'Neill in 1945[1] and the report of the death of Maria Colwell in 1974[2] there had been hardly any similar investigations; or at least few that were published. Indeed, it was not until the death of Maria Colwell that social workers came to be the targets of regular public criticism. One of the reasons for this must certainly be the steady stream of some 40 reports of inquiries into child abuse that have been produced since then.

Three recent inquiries in particular have aroused concern and disquiet: those investigating the deaths of Jasmine Beckford in 1985 and of Kimberley Carlile in 1987 and that, a year later, which was appointed to look into the dramatic increase in the number of children taken into care in Cleveland on the grounds of their having been sexually abused.[3] The first two of these inquiries were chaired by Louis Blom-Cooper QC, and were mainly concerned with the performance of social services departments and with social work practice. Important aspects of each were found to be deficient.

The Beckford Report acknowledged that the staff dealing with the case had 'little or no training' to qualify them for their difficult task, and that 'most of the main actors contributed to the tragedy — social services personnel, medical staff, health visitors and their managers, schools and magistrates'. It was, the report warned, 'both crude and simplistic' to attach blame to social workers alone.[4] Nevertheless, the inquiry did find that the social worker who was directly involved had 'totally misconceived her role . . . in enforcing care orders on two very young children at risk' and that her supervisor 'by her non-intervention in flawed social work . . . was grossly negligent'.[5] These were strong indictments of particular individuals who, some charged, were then used by others as convenient scapegoats.

However, the report of the inquiry painted a more general picture of a social work profession which lacked the competence necessary to ensure the protection of children at risk of abuse. Indeed, several of the recommendations were specifically addressed to this problem. For example, it was maintained that there was 'little hope of increasing the competence of social workers and of increasing the confidence of the public . . . so long as social work education remains sorely under-resourced'. Furthermore, it was argued (along lines already proposed by CCETSW) that 'nothing short of three years is required for the professional training of social workers' in order 'to produce a higher degree of proven competence . . . in relation to particular "specialist" areas . . . and in relation to the statutory duties imposed on social workers'.[6] The inquiry had put social work practice and training under scrutiny and had found them wanting. In doing so it probably contributed to what it implied was a crisis of public confidence in social work.

The report of the inquiry into the death of Kimberley Carlile was published two years later. It followed similar lines and, again, whilst finding that the two key social workers and the two health visitors had 'failed in a number of respects to apply the standard of skill that could be objectively expected',[7] explained that its criticism had to be tempered by other considerations.

Too much was expected of particular individuals in 'an inherently defective system' at a time of severe constraint on resources (rate capping) and in the face of a sudden surge in referrals of children at risk.

More generally, the report questioned the form that such inquiries should take. It concluded that 'where the cases arouse no particular public concern, the investigation should be conducted by the Local Ombudsman or the Area Review Committee's standing panel of inquiry'. This, the report continued, 'should be the main forum for child abuse inquiries until the relevant professional bodies, working in collaboration, can take over the task . . . *For that to happen a General Council of Social Work will have to be established*'[8] (emphasis added). As well as this specific recommendation it was also proposed that 'agreement be reached concerning the minimum expectations of the social worker at the point of qualification' and that, to this end, CCETSW 'should oversee continuing discussion between those organising courses and employers to dovetail their respective responsibilities for the standard of service provided'.[9]

These two widely publicised reports imparted a considerable impetus to the public debate about social work competence, its relationship to training and also to the question of how apparent failures in practice should be investigated. Clearly, the Carlile Report had in mind that not only would a General Social Work Council assume responsibility for regulating the profession but also for undertaking inquiries that went beyond the conduct of any single individual.

The inquiry into child abuse in Cleveland in 1987 chaired by Lord Justice Butler-Sloss followed intense media reporting and was accompanied by a considerable public interest.[10] Although the actions and decisions of the paediatricians involved attracted most attention, there was also an outcry that social workers had been too ready to acquiesce in taking into care children who had been diagnosed as having been sexually abused. The report made clear, however, that there were understandable reasons for what they did; in particular, there was the influence of the mounting criticism of social workers for not removing children at risk that had followed previous inquiries. Together with this there was the fact that social workers were confronted with firm medical diagnoses combined with urgent requests from the paediatricians that they should apply for place of safety orders.

Although the social services department was criticised for certain failures, especially those connected with its poor relationship with the police, the inquiry's conclusion was that no social workers acted 'other than in good faith' and that they had done 'their best under great pressure and in stressful conditions'. Nevertheless, their 'resources of manpower, skill and experience' were considered to be inadequate 'to deal with the height of the crisis'.[11] Once again better and more specialised training was recommended.

All three reports (together with many others) certainly contributed to a sense of public disquiet about social work, linked with a wish to see it better regulated. However, they also demonstrated how complicated the patterns of responsibility and action were. Although individuals may have erred in their judgements and left undone things that should have been done, they did so within organisational and managerial settings that left much to be desired. Furthermore, each of the reports made clear that the social workers were not always adequately trained and supported for the work that they were being asked to do — a view echoed by CCETSW in its 1987 report *Care for Tomorrow*.[12]

The inquiries highlighted the indispensability of professional skill and judgement to good practice, whilst at the same time showing that the question of accountability went beyond the behaviour of any single person. In doing so they captured one of the reasons for the anxiety that some have expressed about the creation of a General Council; namely, that by only having power to discipline those people whom it registered it might deal with them in ways that divorced their conduct or performance from the circumstances in which they were obliged to work. If that happened the idea of public accountability (or corporate accountability) stood in danger of being sacrificed to the cause of professional accountability.

Such apprehension may have been somewhat diminished by the tone of the latest report of Elizabeth Newson QC, on the death of Liam Johnson. It protested that it was both misleading and dangerous to assume 'that all violence to children is predictable and preventable'.[13] It placed no blame upon any social worker and laid greater emphasis than usual upon the culpability of the perpetrators. 'Children die, sometimes tragically, and sometimes at the hands of those who should care for them. Responsibility for these deaths lies overwhelmingly with those who kill them, not with those whose role has been to try to help the family.' The report also questioned whether, every time a child known to the social services is abused or killed, that automatically there should be an inquiry: 'if we have reached a stage at which even limited contact with social services is sufficient to raise a hunt for scapegoats, the implications for those services are appalling'.[14]

Since the publication of the review of the Liam Johnson case at the end of November 1989, other instances of children being killed have been reported in the press. In the two latest, comments were made to the effect that no social worker was to blame for what happened. The prosecution made this clear in the case of a foster mother who killed a baby girl who had been placed in her care,[15] and investigators for the London Borough of Ealing into the death of Christopher Palmer at the hands of his teenage father concluded that: 'while in places we have questioned particular elements of staff thinking, there was never a point at which we felt serious professional errors occurred'.[16]

If such statements reflect the emergence of more measured attitudes towards the nature of a social worker's responsibility and accountability, they may encourage a more dispassionate public consideration of what they can be expected to do, and therefore of what needs to be done if they fall short in their performance. Whatever the balance of public opinion becomes, however, there is no doubt that the spate of child abuse inquiries has made the question of the competence of social workers a matter of much greater public concern than hitherto.

Yet the issue is more complicated than this implies. A string of inquiries has also addressed the problem of the abuse of neglect of people by care staff. For example, the report on scandals in residential centres that Roger Clough prepared for the Wagner committee set out the evidence that had accumulated from a selection of inquiries into the maltreatment of adults and children.[17] The crucial difference between these cases and those involving child abuse is that the people perpetrating the abuse were members of staff, albeit that there were usually also grave deficiencies in management that permitted negligent or cruel practices to arise and persist.

However, one of the problems identified by several of the inquiries, but especially those into Nye Bevan Lodge (a home for elderly people run by the London Borough of Southwark) and the more general investigation into establishments in Camden,[18] was that the local authorities' own disciplinary procedure had become virtually unenforceable. For instance, the Camden inquiry reported that because of employment practices that were designed to protect staff, some were kept in care posts for which they were palpably unfitted. Furthermore, delays had occurred in dealing with complaints and there were instances where staff who were found guilty of serious misconduct were transferred rather than dismissed. This, the report maintained, had given rise to the 'belief that almost any misconduct will be condoned and that senior staff are helpless to take effective disciplinary action even for violence, serious neglect of duty, openly abusive behaviour and refusal to obey reasonable orders'.[19]

There is no doubt that the reports of inquiries into the maltreatment of people in residential homes for the elderly, mental handicap hospitals and community homes for children (together with the media attention that they have received) have added another dimension to the issue of the protection of vulnerable clients, especially those who find themselves dependent upon staff employed to provide the intimate day-to-day care that they are unable to provide for themselves. It is not simply a matter of incompetence but of misconduct. We do not know how widespread that is, but its identification is certainly complicated by the rapid growth in the private residential sector. Residents in private homes are not immune from ill-treatment or neglect as the cases coming before the Residential Homes Tribunal indicate.[20] Nor is the problem restricted to residential care: day care and domiciliary care have to be considered as well.

This is not to say that incompetence is a social work phenomenon and misconduct something that happens in care situations; obviously not. These issues have risen to the surface differently and for different reasons in the two settings. However, the evidence of maltreatment, insensitive or inappropriate care in residential homes *is* a compelling reason for the inclusion of social care staff in any national system of standard-setting, registration and discipline. If the principal justification for a General Council is the protection of the public (and especially the vulnerable public) then, simply in quantitative terms, the care sector cannot be disregarded.

Chapter 6

COMMUNITY CARE

The movement for the expansion of community care has gathered considerable momentum since 1980, especially in the last four or five years. The details of this development have been extensively documented and discussed.[1] Here it is only necessary to identify the key features of these changes that are relevant to the arguments for and against some form of General Council.

The desire to reduce the amount of hospital provision for long-stay patients, especially for the mentally ill, the mentally handicapped and the elderly, has been a powerful motive for the development of community care. Although progress was at first relatively slow, and it continues to be uneven, the shift of responsibility from the health services to the social services that this has entailed has been considerable, albeit the extent to which it has been possible to discharge that responsibility leaves much to be desired. The picture is further complicated because the reduction in the long-term use of hospitals for the elderly has occurred alongside the dramatic increase in the provision of places in private residential homes and nursing homes.[2] Nevertheless, the fact remains that there are now many more frail, handicapped and disabled people living in the community or in residential homes or hostels for whom social services staff bear some responsibility.

This change has meant that more social workers are having to help to support more people in settings which do not protect them from the risks and hazards to which their dependencies expose them. Their needs are often complex: the appropriate resources are scattered and scarce. Increasingly social workers are being expected to act as case managers, assessing need and risk, mobilising resources, co-ordinating an assortment of contributions and monitoring what happens. Certainly, the notion of case management figures prominently in the government's latest community care white paper.[3] It will be closely linked to the 'assessment of need'; especially in relation to the need for admission to residential care. Over and above this, however, the government 'sees considerable merit' in there being a case manager who is nominated to take responsibility for ensuring that individuals' needs are regularly reviewed, resources are managed effectively and 'that each service user has a single point of contact'.[4] Such developments will invest certain social service staff (possibly drawn from a variety of organisations) with more explicit power, both to arrange and to deny services. It will increase the responsibility for what they do, even though they may be guided by senior colleagues. As CCETSW has pointed out, the success of community care policies 'depends on having workers who are able to appraise fully the risks to their clients and others of maintaining them in the community'.[5]

The centrality of the problem of assessing and managing risk is even more clearly apparent in the sustained quest for community sentences for offenders and in the development of the parole system.[6] Similarly, in the child care field there has been a growing use of placements 'home on trial' (which allow children who are subject to a care order to be returned home without the order having been discharged) for those who have been committed to care because they have been neglected or abused.[7] The risk associated with such policies are obvious. At the same time social workers have been encouraged to avoid the necessity of admitting children to care. This has made heavy demands upon time and other resources; but it has also meant that social workers are required to exercise fine judgements, again often at the borderline of high risk. The extent to which preventive strategies have been successfully implemented is reflected in the dramatic reduction (by a quarter) in the number of children in care during the 1980s. However, these children have not disappeared; many of them would now be subject to supervision orders, to voluntary supervision whilst they remain at home and to inclusion on 'at risk' registers. The changes introduced by the 1989 Children's Act seem likely to lead to there being more children in such situations and therefore to even greater demands being made on the exercise of exacting judgements by social workers.

In their various guises community care and preventive policies have increased the level of expectation of what social workers should and can do. New and heavier responsibilities have been placed upon them. That may lead some to imagine that the task in residential settings has become proportionately less demanding. There is no evidence that this has happened. Indeed, demographic changes plus, for example, efforts to enable the elderly to remain at home as long as possible, have meant that many residential homes are now looking after a higher proportion of frail, confused and handicapped residents than ever before. As the Griffiths Report on community care pointed out in 1988, because the current presumption is that people should 'be helped to stay in their own homes as long as possible', residential, nursing home and hospital care comes to be 'reserved for those whose needs cannot be met in any other way'.[8] Similarly, as more of those who can be are kept out of penal establishments, out of community homes for children or out of homes for the disabled, so those who are admitted or remain are likely to have more concentrated and more deep-seated needs.

Staff working in day care services have also been affected by the pursuit of policies for community care, especially since the needs of informal carers have gained a foothold on the political agenda. Day centres of all kinds are being expected to make a more significant contribution by offering respite, training and occupation. Many of those whom they now serve would have been residents in long-stay hospitals or homes ten years ago. These changes are universally applauded; but they place greater demands and more onerous responsibilities upon the staff.

Whilst this assortment of changes has been taking place there has also been, as we have seen, a growing insistence that those who exercise professional discretion should become more accountable for what they do or do not do. However, it is not always easy to determine at what level of any social service organisation this accountability is supposed to be located. Nor is it always clear to whom the social worker is expected to be accountable: to the client (or potential client); to the employing organisation; to their profession or to a more generally conceived 'public'. However, it may be that they are accountable to all these groups, albeit in different ways. Some social work staff obviously feel that they are becoming increasingly trapped in a web of mixed and often contradictory expectations.

There are two ways of looking at how these developments affect the argument about the need for a General Council. On the one hand there is the view that because social workers and social care staff are increasingly being expected to deal with issues of risk and vulnerability, that the case for their performance being subject to external scrutiny and regulation is substantially strengthened. Furthermore, since the successful pursuit of community care (and other policies as well for that matter) depends upon the co-operation of various agencies and individuals there is, it is argued (especially, as we have seen, by the BMA), a pressing need for a General Council that establishes who is considered to be competent in what fields, and that clarifies the kinds of standards of conduct to which those whom it registers subscribe.

The alternative view is that as heavier responsibilities are placed upon them and as they are expected to assume a greater personal accountability, social services staff will become increasingly exposed to the risk of being scapegoated. If staff are denied adequate training, have insufficient resources at their disposal and are poorly served by upper management, then the level of their accountability should be lowered accordingly. Unless appropriate means exist for distinguishing professional from corporate responsibility and for imposing accountability in each case, then, it is argued, the idea of a General Council that is concerned only with registered individuals should be resisted.

On the face of it this second interpretation looks to be mainly concerned about the fate of staff and, that being so, it has to be surrendered in favour of the first, once the test of what is in the public's best interest is applied. However, that conclusion is too simple. The public (or users') interest may be ill-served if the opportunity to regulate individual practitioners obscures the existence of grave shortcomings within the system. Scapegoating will not only injure the scapegoat but also weaken the prospect of the true problem being recognised and addressed. Moreover, the fear of being unfairly held responsible for actions and events over which they have little control is likely to lower staff morale, and that is hardly a recipe for high quality service.

Thus, as far as the case for a General Council is concerned, the implications of the policy developments and the demands on practice that have been described in this chapter are by no means self-evident. However, the balance of the argument may well turn upon the likelihood of there being a satisfactory means of distinguishing individual responsibility (and therefore accountability) from that of corporate bodies or groups, and beyond that upon whether a Council were given the authority to comment both on individual performance, competence or conduct and upon the policies, resources and structures of the employing agency. These matters are considered further in Part 3.

Chapter 7

THE INDEPENDENT SECTOR

It has already been noted that one of the longstanding arguments against a General Council is that its regulative functions would usurp (or at least duplicate) those exercised by local authorities as employers. The assumption lying behind this objection is that since local government is a democratic system the interests of those who use its services are protected by their elected members. There is the further presumption that the appointment and subsequent control of staff by public employers safeguards the interests of users because the provision of such services is guided by reference to a public rather than to any private interest. That argument cannot be applied to the so-called independent sector services since, by definition, they are not public and their management cannot be held accountable to an electoral constituency.

Until the 1980s, the private sector of welfare was small. Since then parts of it have expanded dramatically. For example, the number of places in private residential homes for the elderly increased threefold between 1980 and 1989 and there has been approximately the same rate of growth in the number of beds in private nursing homes, clinics and hospitals.[1] The reason for this extraordinary multiplication is to be found in the changes that were made to the supplementary benefit scheme in 1980 and 1983 which, through the system of board and lodging allowances, amounted to the introduction of an open-ended subsidy that created a popular market for these services that did not exist before.[2]

Unfortunately, as has been pointed out, next to nothing is known about the composition or even the precise size of the workforce in this private residential sector; but if the number of places has grown by a factor of three during the 1980s it would be reasonable to assume that the number of staff of all kinds has increased by the same proportion. Indeed, in England and Wales at least, it is likely that their number now exceeds the number employed by local authorities in their residential homes. For example, the Firth working party estimated that in Great Britain in 1986 there were 10,000 managers and 27,000 care staff in private homes[3], and the Webb committee calculated that there was probably a net annual growth rate of 15 per cent amongst the former and 17 per cent among the latter.[4] If these rates have continued to apply, then in 1989 there were over 15,000 managers and over 43,000 care staff. There are no up-to-date figures for the comparable local authority residential services but it is unlikely that they now employ more than 12,000 senior staff and 35,000 care assistants.[5]

Whereas regulations exist concerning the employment of a certain number of registered nurses in private nursing homes, there is no such requirement with respect to residential homes. The only assurance that users or potential users have that the standards of care are satisfactory is through their direct experience or by relying upon the inspection and registration undertaken by the local authorities. The regulations to which the authorities work specify that there should be an 'adequate' number of 'suitably qualified and competent staff'.[6] However, the regulations do not indicate the nature of the qualification or the competence expected; that is left to local interpretation. Indeed, at present a local authority's responsibility is essentially to approve or disapprove a home as a whole. It has no power to discipline staff other than by making an unfit person's dismissal a condition of a home's registration; but the process of assembling the necessary evidence is fraught with difficulties. In practice, therefore, it mainly falls to employers to monitor how well or badly staff do their job and to take any action that they deem necessary in order to make improvements. Doubtless, some managers do these things conscientiously and with care, but there will be others who, for one reason or another, do not. In any case, there remain problems about how the competence of the managers themselves is established and monitored.

Thus, there is a large but unknown pool of staff in private residential care settings whose appointment, performance and training are subject to no systematic and reliable system of regulation short of the operation of market forces and consumer choice. However, in the case of the frail, confused or disabled the value of these sanctions is likely to be severely constrained, particularly once they have become resident.

The general problem that the growth of private residential care has exposed will become more serious, since one of the key objectives set out in the government's white paper *Caring for People* is the promotion of 'a flourishing independent sector alongside good quality public services'.[7] Local authorities will be expected 'to make maximum use of the independent sector' and they will be required to draw up plans to that end which will be subject to ministerial approval.[8] Some local authorities have already moved a considerable distance in this direction by, for example, selling their residential accommodation to private or voluntary organisations: more of them seem likely to follow.

Given the clear and insistent government lead in this matter it must be expected that 'independent' welfare provision of all kinds will proliferate. However, the introduction of public assessment prior to an individual's admission to subsidised private or voluntary residential accommodation, and the transfer to local authorities of part of the responsibility for providing that subsidy, may retard the growth of private homes. Certainly, that seems to be the intention, although it may be confounded by the force of demographic and other pressures.

What is now receiving official encouragement is the expansion of non-residential private and voluntary services which will mostly be purchased, regulated and orchestrated by local authorities. This is equally the theme in the probation field where the recent green paper has made it clear that the service will be expected to look at the whole question of contracting out parts of its work.[9] The kinds of private and voluntary organisations or individuals that secure such contracts is a matter of speculation. Indeed, as in the local authority sphere it is hard to foresee exactly what type of private services will develop; but all of them will be employing staff, at one level or another, whose competence is a crucial factor in determining their quality. Whether the regulatory function of the local authorities or the contractual arrangements with the independent sector that they and the probation service reach will enable them to insist upon the employment of certain staff with specified competences remains to be seen. What happens is likely to vary from place to place, adding further complication.

Government statements tend not to distinguish between the private and voluntary sectors, although they differ in many important respects. There is, for example, a perception that the voluntary societies operate more like public bodies because private interests are subordinate. Unlike the private sector, there has been comparatively little growth of voluntary residential care but developments have taken place in day care and domiciliary services. Moreover, most of the social workers who are employed outside the public sector work for voluntary organisations, not for private enterprises. The National Children's Homes, for example, describe nearly 1,000 of their staff as social workers (of whom 60 per cent have a relevant qualification), and Barnardo's have approaching 800 social work and day care staff combined.[10] As we have seen, attempts have been made to estimate the size and composition of the workforce in the voluntary sector; but with respect to fieldwork staff at least, the Webb committee concluded that although numbers were known to be increasing there was no firm information.[11] On the other hand, drawing on data assembled by the Firth working party and by CCETSW, the committee was able to calculate that in Great Britain in 1986 there were 3,500 managers of voluntary residential homes (40 per cent of whom held a social work qualification) and some 20,000 care staff. The annual net rate of growth in the number of the former was estimated to be three per cent and for the latter 1½ per cent, suggesting that by 1989 there would have been a modest increase to some 3,800 and 21,000 respectively. However, as with the private sector, the staff working in the voluntary sector are not subject to any external regulation, other than indirectly through the local authorities' responsibility for the inspection and registration of homes.

Despite its sparsity there is clear evidence that a substantial body of social work and especially care staff is employed in the private and voluntary sectors of welfare. Responsibility for the monitoring and development of their competence rests almost wholly with a multitude of employers and committees located in many types of organisations. It is no longer possible, therefore, to claim (and it will be even less so in the future) that there is no need for the independent regulation of social work and social care staff because most of them work in a public sector that acts in the public interest and is ultimately held to account through the democratic system.

In the face of a rapidly growing private sector it becomes impossible to invoke the weaker (but common) argument that because most of the staff who work outside public agencies are employed by voluntary bodies (which are sometimes anwerable to an identifiable constituency and almost always to a committee of management), that there is little need for any independent regulation. There is also now a distinct possibility that there will be an increase in the present very small number of self-employed social workers; there are already examples of local authorities and others using the services of social work consultants from this group. It is also notable that there is an increasing number of *guardians ad litem* who provide reports to the courts in certain child care cases. Although some of them are employed by neighbouring local authorities, when they act as guardians they are operating as independent practitioners, albeit appointed by the courts. Furthermore, the planned phasing-out of the divorce court welfare service will create another opening which could well be filled by self-employed social workers.

A greater diversification of employers has accompanied the growth of what is being termed 'welfare pluralism'. In such a fragmented field a variety of different expectations, standards and assumptions will prevail. A General Council, through its functions of registration and regulation, could provide one means whereby a measure of independent and standardised control could begin to be exercised over the employment of what is at present (and likely to be more so in the future) a heterogeneous and unidentifiable workforce.

Chapter 8

NATIONAL VOCATIONAL QUALIFICATIONS

One of the most important new factors to have entered the debate about the need for a Social Work or Social Services Council since 1982 has been the establishment of the National Council for Vocational Qualifications (NCVQ).

From the early part of the 1980s onwards the government expressed a growing concern about the lack of a sufficiently well-trained labour force. This was reinforced by the 1984 Labour Force Survey which showed that 40 per cent of the workforce possessed no qualifications whatsoever.[1] If the country was to compete successfully in world markets, it was argued, it was essential that steps be taken to improve matters. Unless that were done, the nation's economic survival was threatened. The issues were considered in a number of different contexts,[2] but in the white paper *Education and Training for Young People*[3] published in 1985 the government announced that it intended to review vocational qualifications throughout England and Wales. A working group was rapidly assembled under the auspices of the Manpower Services Commission (MSC) and the Department of Education and Science (DES), and reported in 1986.[4] It concluded that 'the most effective way of providing coherence, clearly understood standards and routes of progression' was 'to bring qualifications within a readily understandable national framework'. Moreover, it considered that a vocational qualification should be defined as 'a statement of competence clearly relevant to work'.[5] In the process of obtaining such a vocational qualification an assessment would be made of an individual's skills at specified standards, their relevant knowledge and understanding and their ability to apply these to the performance of relevant tasks. In short, the working group argued, there should be a comprehensive system of vocational qualifications 'based on the assessment of competence' and directly relevant to the needs of employment and the individual'. A framework was recommended that would be based upon broad levels of award.[6]

The implementation of these measures was to become the responsibility of a National Council for Vocational Qualifications. This was seen as a body that

> develops policy for the vocational qualifications system as a whole, negotiates to achieve the stated objectives for the system and accredits those bodies that are approved to offer awards within a new national framework.[7]

It was not to be an examining or validating body, nor was it to be established on a statutory basis.

Barely three months after these recommendations were published the government had accepted them in its white paper *Working Together — Education and Training*.[8] It maintained that there was a need 'to bridge the unhelpful divide between the so-called "academic" and the so-called "vocational" qualification' and that vocational qualifications needed to be related more directly and clearly 'to competence required (and acquired) at work'.[9] It was the intention that rapid progress should be made in establishing a national scheme. The white paper concluded with the rallying cry that its reforms were 'about improving qualifications and therefore standards: standards of performance, of reliability, of quality . . . In the past,' it maintained, 'we have paid too little attention to standards and our expectations have been too low'.[10]

The first four levels of vocational qualifications were to be in place by 1991 and once established the NVCQ set about the task of having competences specified in a large number of fields. Employer and employee-led groups were set up for the purpose, usually enlisting the assistance of advisers or consultants and liaising with the appropriate accrediting bodies. A Care Sector Consortium was formed as one of these groups. It included representatives of the local authorities; the private and voluntary sector employers; the relevant unions; the main training agencies; the principal accrediting bodies and the probation service. The Consortium established various steering groups (with co-opted specialists) to deal with particular areas of employment. Each steering group appointed a project director and field staff to work on the identification, definition and assessment of units of competence.

For the purpose of this report the most important of the steering groups was the one concerned with residential, domiciliary and day care work, although another looking at support work in health care has dealt with overlapping activities.[11] The initial work of the residential, domiciliary and day care group was due to be completed in March 1990. After that the various units of competence, which have now appeared in draft form,[2] will be piloted by a CCETSW-convened group of awarding bodies comprising CCETSW; the Business and Technical Education Council (BTEC); the City and Guilds and the English National Board (for Nursing, Midwifery and Health Visiting). Obviously some of the units will be widely applicable and others of a more specialist nature; different social care jobs at different levels will demand different combinations of units. The joint awarding bodies (as above) are currently considering long-term collaboration in the overseeing and issuing of jointly certificated awards in social care. In Scotland, the Scottish Vocational Education Council (SCOVTEC) and CCETSW have agreed in principle to the joint validation and certification of Scottish vocational competencies endorsed by the Care Sector Consortium.

Many problems are still to be overcome if the scheme is to be successfully implemented. There is the sheer scale of the undertaking; as many as a quarter of a million care staff may be eligible for consideration. Obviously, the task of assessment will have to be undertaken at the local level by employers; but that then raises questions about how, and according to what criteria, their competence to assess is determined. Over and above that there will need to be machinery for external verification and appeal. Not all employers, whether in the public or the independent sectors, will be equally enthusiastic about doing the work, not least because of the cost.

The question of how best to phase the operation will also have to be settled locally and that may well create variations throughout the country during the early years. If, as seems likely, salaries come to be linked (either directly or indirectly) with the possession of a certain level of national vocational qualification then the issue of which staff are dealt with first will become a difficult and sensitive matter. That, in its turn, bears upon the question of how existing qualifications are viewed and whether the adoption of some form of conditional accreditation might threaten to dilute the intended standards.

There is also, of course, the problem of the sorry state of national and local data about the personal social services workforce, particularly in social care, to which the Webb committee attached great importance.[13] The implementation and maintenance of the NVQ system for assessing competence will require speedy and extensive improvements to be made, not least in incorporating into local or regional data bases information about the private and voluntary sectors. Although the LGTB has been developing a workforce analysis system for local application[14] it now seems likely that it will move instead to support the nationwide use of a system developed by the Convention of Scottish Local Authorities (COSLA) which is in the process of being introduced into all Scottish social work departments. If such a system is adopted beyond Scotland, many of the problems of planning for and maintaining the NCVQ's system locally and monitoring it nationally would be substantially eased. It would certainly provide a platform from which the problems of systematic reassessment could be tackled. Competence at particular levels will have to be reviewed from time to time; perhaps every five years. Similarly, if staff are to be able to accumulate units of competence as planned, it will be necessary to have a local record in order to provide a basis for the construction of rolling programmes of assessment.

These are some of the problems that lie ahead. Nonetheless, the NCVQ remains committed to having its scheme (up to level 4) in place and operational by 1991. There are also plans for dealing with the assessment of managerial competence and of extending the scheme above level 4, albeit on a voluntary basis. The additional tier (or tiers) will be referred to as the 'higher' level(s).[15] However, the development of this part of the programme will not be completed until after 1991.

Why exactly is the establishment of this system of national vocational qualifications so important in the discussion about whether or not a General Social Work or Social Services Council is needed or feasible? First, it is directly relevant to the longstanding problem of the large proportion of unqualified care staff. Since the NVQ scheme concentrates upon the determination of competence rather than upon qualification, it provides a means whereby the skill and experience of some unqualified staff can be recognised. Over and above that, however, it is clear that the implementation of the scheme will encourage employees to take advantage of a variety of training opportunities in order to improve their level of competence. Employers, for their part, are likely to inaugurate more systematic training programmes, given the existence of an assessment system that is work-based and which has been designed by an employment-led group. The fact that, so far, both the employers and the unions have lent their support to these developments augurs well for their future success.

Of course, questions immediately arise about the status of particular levels of competence, about the differences between them and about the particular awards that will be available at each level. CCETSW's proposals for the reform of social work and social care training, which are considered more fully in the next chapter, include the establishment of a qualification in social care that would correspond to the NVQ level 3, and there is also a suggestion that there might be a preliminary certificate at level 2 and an advanced certificate that would be equivalent to level 4.[16] Whatever precise details emerge, these developments offer a basis upon which a significant number of care staff, at least at levels 3 and 4, could be included in any system of national registration and regulation that might be devised.

The detailed work on units of competence is the second feature of the NVQ system that is relevant to the debate about the feasibility of a General Social Work or Social Services Council. It has been plain from the outset that any arrangement for registration would have to be based upon more than an individual's possession of a relevant qualification. It would need to reflect their competence in practice; yet the problem of how the competence might be established (as well as by whom and how often) has remained to be resolved. Hitherto, the main proposal has been that there should be two years of supervised practice after qualification with an assessment of competence based upon performance during that period. The most comprehensive analysis of what such assessment might entail was provided by a working party set up by BASW which reported in 1979.[17] However, with the limited resources at its disposal, it was impossible for such a group to develop its ideas in detail. Moreover, it did not necessarily reflect the views of other interests.

The work of the Care Sector Consortium indicates that agreed units of competence can be formulated, are susceptible to being assessed by a variety of methods and, although locally administered, can provide the basis for a national scheme. The emergence of the NVQ and the likelihood of its extension into the 'higher' level(s) has provided both a practical and a political foundation upon which the specification and assessment of competences can actually be developed.

As a broadly-supported initiative, therefore, the NVQ developments have already changed the debate about qualifications and competences in the social services. This is not to say that they automatically strengthen the case for a General Council. It might be argued that with the emergence of the NVQ scheme the need for any other form of registration or accreditation disappears. However, there is no suggestion that the NCVQ will operate any disciplinary procedures or issue codes of conduct or practice, although their competence standards may be drawn upon in the processes of inspection and disciplinary action.

A fuller appreciation of the implication of these developments for the personal social services, however, can be gained from viewing them alongside the proposals for the reform of education and training in social work and social care. These are considered next.

Chapter 9

THE REFORM OF EDUCATION AND TRAINING

CCETSW embarked upon a review of training for social work in the early part of the 1980s. In 1987, it published *Care for Tomorrow* which set out a compelling case for reform and proposed radical changes.[1] From the point of view of the debate about a General Social Work or Social Services Council two of these changes were of considerable significance. First, there was the proposal to merge the Certificate of Qualification in Social Work (CQSW) and the Certificate in Social Service (CSS) into a single professional social work award, obtained after three years' education and training, and to be called the Qualifying Diploma in Social Work (QDSW). Secondly, there was a plan to establish a series of new qualifications in social care based on NCVQ levels of competence that, linked with the QDSW, would form 'a comprehensive and progressive system of training and qualifications . . . based upon credit accumulation'.[2]

The first of these proposals would make clear who was and who was not qualified in social work, although that aim was substantially achieved later in 1987 when CCETSW recognised the CSS as a social work qualification. More important was the intention to raise the standards of social work education and training by, for example, setting the minimum core elements to be included in approved courses, together with the requirement that each student should develop additional understanding and skill in 'an area of special emphasis'. These changes, along with a number of others, would 'prepare social workers properly for accountable professional practice'.[3] Were the reforms to achieve that aim and were they linked additionally to an initial period of supervised and assessed performance in employment, then the case for holding social workers accountable for what they did (or did not do) would be that much stronger. There would be less justification for the claim that the quality and character of training had failed to provide the foundation from which accountable practice could be reasonably expected. There is a more powerful case for the regulation and disciplining of a profession that has been educated and trained to an appropriate standard than of one which has not, for then accountability is clearer.

CCETSW's plans received a setback when, in 1988, the government announced that it was unwilling to fund the third year of training that had been proposed as a basis for the new QDSW. As a result certain matters have had to be reconsidered. Even so, the broad conception of the plan remains in place, but with a two-year Diploma in Social Work (DipSW) replacing the QDSW and provision for at least one further level of post-qualifying award.

The recommendations for the reform of training in social care were, if anything, more important, and were clearly linked to the developments that were foreseen for the determination of care competences within the NVQ framework in England and Wales and SCOVTEC in Scotland. As we have noted, it was suggested that the new qualification in social care should correspond to level 3 of the NVQ with the possibility of a preliminary certificate at level 2 and an advanced certificate at level 4. In line with the principles that informed the NVQ developments, it was proposed that the award of the social care certificate would be related to the assessment of workplace modules of training offering core, specialist and management elements.

The size of the training programme that the new qualifications in social care will demand is large, but as the CCETSW report pointed out, a significant proportion of social care staff has 'already undertaken some form of training', although mostly 'in-service and largely without national acknowledgement of qualification'.[4] For example, a training support programme for staff working with elderly people has been introduced to encourage more in-service training and to improve the training infrastructure within social services departments.

Developed alongside the NVQ these proposals, if successfully implemented, promise to increase the proportion of staff in residential and day care with certified competence. This in turn increases the feasibility of bringing them, along with field social workers, under the umbrella of a General Council. However, the actual impact of the introduction of a new qualification in social care linked with an NVQ level is difficult to calculate. For example, much will depend upon rates of turnover and these might be affected by the fact that the qualification will become part of a progressive system that can lead to a DipSW and beyond. Thus, for some it may become the passport to further training which takes them out of residential or day care into the better remunerated ranks of field social work. On the other hand the creation of a career structure that fans out into all parts of the personal social service system, and of which the new social care qualification will form a part, may both reduce losses through the lack of perceived opportunity and at the same time encourage recruitment.

What is of crucial importance in the impending reform of the education and training of social work and social care staff is the introduction of flexible and alternative routes to qualification and the determination of competence. For example, the expansion of employment-based schemes may encourage private sector employers to provide or accept more opportunities for their staff to be trained, or enable the authorities to be in a position to require them to do so.

An important distinction threads its way through all these deliberations; that is, the difference between demonstrated competence in work and in training. The NVQs are about the former. Training is only one route to acquiring competence and related qualifications. Clearly, CCETSW envisages a system (reflecting NCVQ requirements) that would enable and encourage competent staff to present themselves for assessment for one of the new awards at the appropriate level. Consequently, administrative structures and related costs will have to accommodate two elements: work-based assessment machinery for all those seeking an award, and training provision for all those who need it. Work on the former is being undertaken by the Joint Awarding Bodies as part of the current pilot studies; the cost and organisation of the training is still under discussion.

It is plain that the education and training of social work and social care staff is in the melting pot. Under these circumstances it is not only important to consider how the consequences of that impinge upon the case for a General Council, but also how the establishment of such a body, incorporating CCETSW's function as one of its arms, would affect the results of the transformation — especially in the field of social care.

Chapter 10

THE EUROPEAN DIMENSION

These days any consideration of future developments in whatever field must take into account the opportunities and constraints which derive from membership of the European Community (EC). In the context of the debate surrounding the feasibility of a General Council which would have responsibility for the registration and regulation of social services staff, therefore, it is important to remember that one of the aspirations of the European Community is the free movement of labour between member states. Obviously the central issues which have to be addressed in order to secure agreement on the acceptability or otherwise of people wishing to work in a country other than their own are whether their qualifications are considered to be comparable, and whether their standard of professional conduct can be relied upon. Under the Treaty of Rome the Council of Ministers has been empowered to issue Directives that formulate the criteria upon which member states should make their decisions in these matters, and it has already done so for some professions.[1]

In December 1988 the Council issued a Directive[2] which was designed to apply to professions such as social work that were not covered by earlier pronouncements. This set out a 'general system for the recognition of higher education diplomas awarded on completion of professional education and training of at least three years' duration'.[3] This presented a problem in the United Kingdom where not all social workers, even when qualified, have undergone three years higher education as it appears to be defined.[4] The government's rejection of a three-year training for a QDSW removed the prospect that substantially more will do so in the future. Furthermore, in order for a profession to fulfill the requirements of the Directive it has to be 'regulated', either by the state or, under certain circumstances, by an approved body. Hence, on the counts both of duration of higher education and formal regulation, it seems that most social workers and virtually all social care staff in the United Kingdom fail to satisfy the terms of the Directive by contrast with almost all the other member states.

However, much depends on interpretation; for example, upon exactly how 'three years' of higher education is defined and calculated. CCETSW has argued that three-quarters of those receiving qualifying awards in social work in 1988 did satisfy the criterion of three years' preparation at a university or equivalent level. Likewise, the Council has maintained that social work in the United Kingdom does have the necessary hallmarks of a 'regulated profession'. For instance, the title of 'qualified social worker' is restricted to holders of qualifying awards in social work; probation officers are required to hold the CQSW under the Probation Rules and certain tasks under the Mental Health Act, 1983 (1984 in Scotland) may only be carried out by an 'approved' social worker (a 'mental health officer' in Scotland).

Whether or not the Department of Trade and Industry (DTI), which is the body charged with applying the provisions of the Directive in this country, considers that these specifications are sufficient to satisfy the requirements remains to be seen.

However, a further Directive has recently been issued that aims to extend the effects of the first to those professions for which the training period is less than three years. That will overcome some part of the problem of the duration of education and training; but it does not remove the hurdle of regulation.

Of course, if a General Social Services Council were established both field social work and social care would qualify as regulated professions, but most social care staff would still not meet the higher education requirements of the Directives, and the difference in the standing of the two groups would be widened that much more.

Thus, although the European dimension will become more important, its implications for the debate about a General Council are somewhat ambiguous. Having a regulated profession is a necessary but not sufficient step towards participation in the European professional labour market; but it would provide an important platform from which further negotiations could be conducted.

Although the establishment of a profession regulated by a General Council would bring us closer to the Community norm the question of how many social services staff would meet the other main conditions of the Directives may well affect the pattern of professional migration to and from this country. The more staff who fail to satisfy the Directives' higher education criterion the greater the likelihood that Britain will experience a net immigration of social service professionals, especially if steps are taken to recruit them. As Munday has suggested, 'directors of social services must be keenly interested in . . . the possibilities of recruiting social workers from countries such as Germany where unemployment amongst social workers has been a feature of the 1980s' (for example, 9,000 in 1983).[5] More student and staff exchanges (for example, under the Erasmus programme) could have an important bearing upon the willingness of those who can move to work in another country to do so.

Were an influx of staff from the EC member countries to occur then, as Helen Lockwood speaking on behalf of the SCA has pointed out, its implications for the standard of care would have to be seriously considered.[6] Differences in language, culture, attitudes, styles of training and legislation will all have to be taken into account. Questions of language and attitudes are of the utmost importance in the inter-personal fields in which social work and social care are undertaken. In particular there are issues about competence in English which may have to be carefully defined in relation to specific work: for example, in residential work with the confused elderly; in work with people whose hearing is impaired or with young children whose language development is retarded. At the moment CCETSW scrutinises the acceptability of overseas qualifications for British practice but these are often from English-speaking countries. The scrutiny of many more applicants from member countries of the EC who satisfy the Directive is likely to be a more complicated process for which a General Council could take responsibility.

Chapter 11

SOCIAL SERVICES INSPECTION

With the transfer of responsibility for children's services from the Home Office to the DHSS following the re-organisation of the personal social services in 1970, the former Children's Inspectorate and the social work division of the Department were merged to form the Social Work Service. That brought together organisations of a different size with markedly different modes of operation.[1] In the new service less emphasis was placed upon inspectorial or quality control functions and rather more on providing advice, support and the dissemination of examples of good practice. The style was low-key, informal and private. As the re-organised services in local government settled down and as pressures began to mount for a closer scrutiny of the efficiency and effectiveness of the personal social services, for the better protection of clients' rights, and for the application of tests of 'value for money', so the prevailing approach of the Social Work Service began to be questioned. However, there were mixed pressures. For instance, in 1982 the Barclay committee proposed that an independent inspectorate should be created which would monitor the practice of both social workers and their employing agencies[2] — not, it should be noted, to establish cost effectiveness.

The outcome of these pressures was a statement by the Secretary of State in 1985 that, following agreement with the local authority associations, a Social Services Inspectorate (SSI) would be established which had 'professional obligations to the people who need and use the social services'.[3] It was to consist of existing members of the Social Work Service augmented by additional staff drawn from a variety of backgrounds, including those concerned with management and the measurement of performance. Its task was to 'assist local authorities to obtain value for money through the efficient and economic use of available resources'. Furthermore, its aim would be 'to help to secure the most effective use of professional and other resources, normally by identifying good practice and spreading knowledge about it'.[4] There could be formal inspection initiated by ministers or by the Department, but clearly it was expected that most of the work would be done without the use of formal powers.

The new Inspectorate came into operation in April 1985. Its responsibilities were more precisely defined than before, its resources enlarged and its professional skills widened. An annual work programme was inaugurated and inquiries were undertaken on a range of services and issues. The press began to take notice and, particularly in the last year or so, there has been a steady stream of reports, some sharply critical, that have provided important material upon which improvements could be based.

Changes are also afoot in the Probation Inspectorate which has already been re-organised as a result of an 'efficiency scrutiny' in 1987. The recent green paper proposes that it should become statutorily based; that is, that it should have an existence independent of a purely departmental one. Furthermore, it is suggested that the powers and duties of the Inspectorate should not be restricted to the probation service. 'If voluntary and private sector organisations are to be more involved in the delivery of community-based penalties and other work with offenders, the remit of the Inspectorate might be extended to cover any such work funded by the Government'.[5] In addition, all probation areas will have to have 'internal monitoring and inspection' procedures in place by the autumn of 1990.

Other developments in local inspection have already occurred in social services departments. Largely in response to the growth in the number of private residential homes, local authorities were given wider powers and duties in connection with the inspection and registration of these homes under the provisions of the Registered Homes Act, 1984. This inevitably raised questions about the comparability of standards in private and local authority establishments and led to various proposals that a more independent inspectorate should be created. Such a view was put forward by the National Council of Voluntary Organisations (NCVO) in 1986.[6] In 1988 the Wagner committee on residential care also recommended that all sectors should be subject to the same system of registration and inspection and that no agency should undertake the inspection of its own establishments. It suggested that inspection should be based on an element of peer review.[7] In 1989 a joint ADSS and SCA working group reporting on the regulation of residential services considered that there should be a group of inspectors in each local authority 'managed by a Senior Officer not directly responsible for the delivery of residential care'.[8] Close on the heels of these proposals came the government's statement in its recent white paper *Caring for People,* that 'local authorities will be required to establish inspection and registration units at arm's length from the management of their own services, which will be responsible for checking on standards in both their own homes and independent sector residential care homes'.[9]

As we saw earlier, the Barclay committee suggested that a reformed inspectorate, together with other measures, offered an alternative to the creation of a General Social Work Council as a means of protecting the public interests in the personal social services. Much of what the committee foresaw as following from a reformed inspectorate has been achieved. Yet neither the SSI nor the Probation Inspectorate is constituted so as to deal with cases of individual incompetence or misconduct; that is not their purpose. However, the question remains as to whether, and if so to what extent, the case for a General Council is strengthened or weakened by the changing character of inspection.

A General Council that could be relieved of the need to embrace broader functions connected with the enhancement of standards might appear to some to be both a more attractive and more feasible proposition. For others that would remove a telling argument in its favour. What view is taken will depend upon how the strengths and weaknesses of the case for a General Council are seen in the first place, but also upon the confidence inspired by the inspectorial process. In my view the developments in inspection since the Barclay committee reported in 1982 leave the balance of the argument largely unaffected, except insofar as they bear upon the number of functions that a General Council might be expected to accept over and above professional regulation.

However, it has been suggested that the work of the SSI might become an integral part of a General Council's activities.[10] That would involve an alteration in the constitution of the Inspectorate, particularly in its relationship to the Minister and to the Department of Health. Nonetheless, the fact that all central government departments are now required to consider which parts of their operations can be 'floated off' as quasi-autonomous agencies may cast the future organisational status of the Inspectorate into some doubt. Under these circumstances its incorporation within a General Council may attract a significant measure of political support.

So far, the issue of inspection has been discussed without reference to the contribution of audit. Important changes have also occurred in this field, principally as a result of the Local Government Finance Act, 1982, which resulted from the report of the Layfield committee.[11] Layfield had recommended that there should be an audit service that was independent of both central and local government. This was accepted and achieved through the creation of the Audit Commission for Local Authorities in England and Wales (there is a similar Accounts Commission in Scotland). The Commission began its work in 1983 and now covers the NHS as well as local authorities. Amongst other things it is responsible for the appointment of auditors. The District Audit Service (whose statutory responsibilities were transferred to the Commission from the Department of the Environment) receive a majority of the appointments but private firms are also used. The Commission's ambitious aims are to improve value for money; encourage good management; promote the public interest; monitor performance, and facilitate co-ordination between different agencies. Its approach is illustrated in the case of the personal social services by the critical examination of community care that was published in 1986.[12] In many ways this and other reports were similar to what might have been produced by the Inspectorate; certainly they highlighted deficiencies in both policy and practice as well as making suggestions for improvement.

Somewhat parallel changes in audit functions have occurred at central government level. In 1984 the new National Audit Office replaced the former Exchequer and Audit Department. However, it remains concerned with the scrutiny of central departments and other non-governmental bodies that are substantially funded from public sources in order to secure value for money.

Although of considerable importance in their own right, these changes in the emphasis and organisation of public sector auditing resemble those in the sphere of inspection insofar as arguments about a General Council are concerned. Audits do not deal with individual performance or with the private or voluntary sectors. Even so, the changing role of audit was part of the new climate of the 1980s and appears to be set to play an even more important part in shaping policy and practice in the 1990s; and that must affect the kind of General Council around which the arguments should now revolve.

Chapter 12

THE LOCAL COMMISSIONERS FOR ADMINISTRATION

In this and the next chapter we turn to consider the two major means by which complaints can be made about local social services and look at the extent to which a General Council with investigative and disciplinary power would duplicate what already exists.

Legislation passed in 1974 (1975 for Scotland) established the Commission for Local Administration with five Local Commissioners (or 'Ombudsmen'); three to share responsibility for the work in England and one each for Wales and Scotland.[1] The importance of the Ombudsmen to the question of whether a General Social Work or Social Services Council is required resides in the claim that it would provide a much needed opportunity for complaints against practitioners to be made and investigated. It is also important to consider the functions of the Local Commissioners because one of the general arguments against a Council having disciplinary powers is that since the Ombudsmen are already available to deal with many of the allegations that are likely to arise, and that they could also conduct general inquiries, a Council would not be required to fulfil these roles.

As described in the report of the Widdicombe committee of inquiry into local authority business,[2] the task of the local Ombudsmen is 'to consider complaints from the public that they have suffered an injustice as a result of maladministration by a local authority'.[3] The title of the Commission is therefore significant, since it serves to remind us that its jurisdiction extends only to issues of local authority administration. The committee of inquiry, noting that 'maladministration is not defined in the legislation', gave a list of factors which that term covered. They included 'neglect, bias, unfairness, incompetence and excessive delay', and stated that 'in most cases (maladminstration) amounts to a failure to follow the proper procedures'.[4] A booklet produced by the Commission to explain to members of the public the procedures for and rules about bringing a complaint put it more simply: 'the Local Ombudsmen are not there to question what a Council have done just because someone does not agree with the Council. There must be a complaint that something went wrong, causing injustice to the person who had complained.'[5]

An Ombudsman cannot act unless a complaint is formally referred to him. Initially it was stipulated that only in exceptional circumstances could complaints be brought other than through a councillor, but the Local Government Act of 1988 changed this rule to enable members of the public to take complaints directly to their Local Ombudsman, whereupon complaints rose by 44 per cent. However, the Ombudsman's jurisdiction is restricted in other ways. A complaint cannot be accepted for consideration if there is an alternative means (such as through the courts or a tribunal) by which it might be dealt with; if it is submitted outside a 12 months time limit (unless the Ombudsman considers it reasonable to do so); if it affects all or most of the inhabitants of an area; if it is a personnel matter; or if it concerns an internal matter of management within a school or college. Another restriction on the acceptance of complaints which relate to the actions of local authorities 'in connection with the investigation or prevention of crime' was recently lifted. Although an Ombudsman is required to issue a 'further' report to a local authority which has failed to act upon the recommendations contained in his first report to it on a case, he has no power of enforcement (although since 1988 the authority must respond within three months, notifying the Ombudsman what action it proposes to take).

In its annual report for England for the year 1988-9, the Commission stated that its main objective was 'the investigation of complaints of injustice arising from maladministration by local, water and police authorities, with a view to securing, where appropriate, satisfactory redress for the complainant and better administration for the authorities'.[6] The bulk of complaints brought have always been concerned with planning and housing and 1988-9 was no different in this respect, these subjects representing between them 70 per cent of all those referred during the year. As far as social services departments were concerned, the Local Ombudsmen, as in previous years, received comparatively few complaints (241 or 3.4%). Nevertheless, this figure is increasing, possibly because of the publicity given to inquiries into cases of child abuse.[7] Support for this view came from the Local Ombudsman for the North who, although noting that she had not received any complaints from Cleveland, believed that the publicity surrounding the inquiry into child sexual abuse there 'was responsible for a rise in the number of complaints made . . . from elsewhere about the way social services departments had carried out their responsibilities toward the younger, older and disadvantaged members of the community'.[8] A possible development which might increase the Commission's involvement with social service issues was suggested in the report of the committee of inquiry into the death of Kimberley Carlile; namely, that in future such inquiries might be undertaken by the Local Ombudsman.[9] Of course, similar investigations are already carried out where there is a formal complaint and it was noted in their 1987-8 report that the proposal 'had long been supported by the Commission and was recommended by the Widdicombe committee' which inquired into the conduct of local authority business.[10] However, in an accompanying footnote on the subject, the Commissioner's annual report seems to indicate that it is unlikely that such a development will occur since the Representative Body[11] has 'consistently opposed the Commission being able to initiate investigations without having received a formal complaint' and that it has been supported in that opposition by successive Secretaries of State.[12]

The vast majority of the complaints brought to the Commission (of which, as we have seen, only a very small percentage concern social services departments) do not reach the stage of being formally investigated. At the discretion of the Local Ombudsman most of them are not pursued beyond the stage at which the local authority's detailed comments on the case are considered. Additionally, in a small number of cases the Local Ombudsmen find that the complaint should have been directed elsewhere. Eventually, for example, only 302 cases were formally investigated in 1988-9, and only 14 of these concerned social services departments. Maladministration causing injustice was found in nine instances; in two maladministration without injustice and in the remaining three no maladministration was discovered.

The 1987-88 annual report outlines five cases where maladministration by a social services department was found. Three of these could best be described as failures in communication. One was of a mother who was not given proper advice about her rights of access to her child in care; another involved a disabled person who was not provided with guidance and advice on home adaptations; and the third was a failure to report to the complainants an incident involving their mother which led to her being admitted to hospital from the old people's home where she was a resident. One of the remaining two examples was of maladministration in the way a child was taken into care; and the other concerned the loss of some possessions belonging to a child in care.[13]

The Commission took the opportunity to record in its annual report its concern that, despite efforts to publicise its existence and functions, 'there are still many people who are in the dark about how to seek remedies for injustice', including 'a silent and vulnerable minority who can become victims of local government lapses like anyone else but who are often less able to do anything about them'. Amongst other steps the Commission is taking to improve access to local Ombudsmen, therefore, is to 'discuss with voluntary organisations how they might best assist people who may have difficulty making a complaint because they are young, old or handicapped, or otherwise disadvantaged'.[14] Many of these people are likely to be (or to become) clients of social services departments.

It is clear that the role of the Ombudsmen for local government is limited in important ways by the condition that those cases they investigate must be matters of maladministration or be associated with maladministration. Poor professional practice unconnected with maladministration does not come within their jurisdiction. Of course, what constitutes maladministration is a matter for interpretation and local authorities who dispute an Ombudsman's judgement can seek a judicial review of his report on the grounds that he has not acted in accordance with this requirement; that is, that he has dealt with matters that concerned the exercise of the local authority's proper discretion and which lay outside the question of maladministration.[15]

Furthermore, of course, the local Ombudsman's powers do not extend to the voluntary or private sectors or to other public services, although in some of the latter, such as the health service, there are also commissioners with similar responsibilities but working in a separate administration and bound by different legislation. There has also been a growth of private sector Ombudsmen (such as those for the building societies and insurance industry) and others are promised; for example, a new one for legal services.

Given the limitations upon what an Ombudsman is permitted to investigate it seems clear that the functions envisaged for a General Council are different, although there may certainly be some overlap, particularly if both bodies were to be given the power to conduct general inquiries such as those in child abuse cases. Even with the wider public access to the Ombudsmen that the reforms of 1988 have provided, the argument that their existence undermines the case for a General Council is unconvincing.

Chapter 13

LOCAL COMPLAINTS

The 1980s witnessed a mounting pressure for better complaints procedures to be provided in various fields. We appear to be in the midst of significant changes in attitude towards clients' rights and thus to their complaints. 'Consumerism' is too glib a term to describe what is occurring and why, but it does indicate the direction of the shift that is taking place. Neither central nor local government have remained unaffected. For example, in 1987 the LGTB, with the backing of the unions and the local authority associations, published a call for action in *Getting Closer to the Public*.[1] More specific proposals were put forward with respect to the personal social services throughout the 1980s. At the start of the decade BASW produced *Clients are Fellow Citizens*.[2] This was followed in 1984 by a report from a working party set up by the National Council for Voluntary Organisations (NCVO)[3] and then, in 1988, by the conclusions of another working party established jointly by the National Consumer Council (NCC) and the National Institute for Social Work (NISW).[4] Numerous conferences on the issue were organised.[5] It was plain that in general, and more particularly in the personal social services, the question of consumer (or client) rights had secured a firm foothold on political and professional agendas.

The question is whether, as far as complaints against practitioners in the social services are concerned, these developments make it less necessary for there to be a General Council to which the public and others are able to take allegations of serious professional transgressions. The first consideration must be whether such widespread support and encouragement for the improvement of complaints procedures have been translated into their availability on the ground.

Two major pieces of research provided disappointing evidence. In 1985 the National Consumer Council conducted a survey of complaints procedures in social services departments in England and Wales. This showed that the majority of authorities had no formal procedures that covered all aspects of the personal social services. Furthermore, many authorities had no formal or written procedures.[6] A more general study undertaken by the Centre for Criminological and Socio-Legal Studies at Sheffield University in 1984-6 (but only in England) told a similarly sorry story, even though more social services departments had complaints procedures than other local departments.[7] Half of the responding authorities claimed to have a formal complaints procedure (that is, a written statement) that covered all aspects of the work of their social services department, and another 16 per cent had formal procedures for certain aspects (such as children in care or residential accommodation). Overall two-thirds of the authorities that responded had some kind of formal procedure — although only half publicised them.[8] As the authors of the report point out, it is likely that the non-respondents would not have shown up well.

These were findings from 1986. Whether matters have changed since then is difficult to know, although there certainly appears to have been a flurry of activity in the last year or so, encouraged by the SSI, by the ADSS and by other bodies pressing for improvements. Certainly there have been serious attempts in many areas to encourage the participation of users and to develop more open systems of administration. Certain legislative changes, such as the Disabled Persons' (Services, Representation and Consultation) Act, 1986 and the Children's Act, 1989, will also move practice in that direction.

Notwithstanding the findings of the Sheffield study, complaints procedures in social services departments in 1986 were almost certainly better than at the start of the 1980s, and are likely to have improved further since then. Indeed, the government intends that it should be a statutory requirement for all local authorities to have complaints procedures for child care and for residential care for adults, and probably for day and field services as well.

Virtually every recent report dealing with the field has called for improvements. The Wagner committee on residential care is a good example. In its report it was argued that 'in order to provide some built-in protection for users' rights we consider that each residential services provider must have a clear and well-publicised complaints system to which users can turn when they are dissatisfied . . ."[9] More specifically the committee recommended that such systems should be as readily available in the private and voluntary sectors as in the public.

This directs attention to the need to ensure that adequate complaints procedures exist across a welfare field that is quickly expanding beyond the realms of local government. It may be that the availability of such procedures will be made one of the conditions for the registration of homes, for the approval of contracts, or for the provision of subsidies. If that happens then a regulating local authority can hardly provide less adequate arrangements than it demands for others.

To return to our opening question: how far does this change (and there is still a credibility gap between the rhetoric and the reality) affect the arguments for or against a General Council that would also offer a means of complaint? With one important proviso, I believe that it strengthens the case. Better local complaints procedures mean that more grievances and dissatisfactions can be dealt with at that level. In their absence other systems are likely to attract a greater volume of complaints, and complaints that are not necessarily appropriate to their jurisdictions. Inundation then occurs, and with it public disenchantment. Without adequate local systems of complaint, the complaints procedure of a General Council could well fall into disrepute.

The proviso to this conclusion, however, is that the jurisdictions of the various systems have to be clarified and in terms that the public can understand. That entails first, the definition and classification of complaints (no easy matter); secondly, agreement about the nature of the different jurisdictions; and thirdly, agreement about the routing of complaints between them. These matters are helpfully addressed in the NCC and NISW publication *Open to Complaints*. For example, it is emphasised that it is essential

> to distinguish between professional social work decisions and actions, which could be open to specific forms of scrutiny and challenge, and those aspects of social services provision concerned with the allocation of scarce resources according to criteria of

eligibility and need established by political decisions . . . This is the difference between social work activities and social services provision.

When this difference is not clear it leads 'to confusion about where complaints should be directed'.[10]

Unless crucial distinctions like these are acknowledged and understood, the delusion that all complaints can and should be dealt with by a single system will continue to pass unchallenged. A single system might be desirable at a preliminary stage — with a single local complaints officer helping people to prepare and route their complaints towards the system where there is the greatest likelihood of their being addressed, resolved or redressed. But beyond that, when more formal procedures are invoked, differentiation is necessary because accountability is differentiated.

This is recognised in, for example, the existence of statutory local Housing Benefit Review Boards and Education Appeal Committees. There is likely to be a new class of complaints and appeals once the assessment of the need for financially supported admission to private or voluntary homes is introduced in accordance with the proposal in the government's community care white paper.[11] Most of these will have to be dealt with locally by social services departments — possibly through new residential assessment appeal boards. This probability not only raises questions about the type of local procedure that should be available for different kinds of complaints (independent, departmental, formal or informal), but also serves to emphasise the inevitability of differentiation.

Once this principle is accepted it may be easier to recognise a distinction between the employers' disciplinary jurisdiction and a professional jurisdiction. The NCC-NISW report has made a start by suggesting what the relationship should be between complaints and employer disciplinary procedures. For example, it is commendably direct in recommending that where there is

> a *prima facie* case of abuse or malpractice, the authority should inform the client, stop the complaints procedure, and initiate disciplinary procedures. In less serious cases, the complaints procedure should run its course to enable the client to receive redress; and then afterwards, if appropriate, disciplinary proceedings should be initiated.[12]

Even so, the report was at pains to point out the need for such matters to be negotiated in advance, especially with the unions. The rights of staff also need to be protected. These principles must apply equally to the formulation of the disciplinary functions that a General Council would exercise. In addition it would be imperative for agreement to be reached with the employer interests about disciplinary jurisdictions and about the procedures for cross-referral. This longstanding problem might have a better chance of being resolved when the principle of complaints differentiation comes to be more fully accepted locally. At the very least, the greater emphasis upon citizens' rights is obliging everyone to think more carefully and more precisely about how best they can be respected and protected.

Chapter 14

A REVIEW

The examination of the principal factors that, since 1982, were likely to have affected the balance of the argument about the desirability and feasibility of a General Council now need to be summarised and the implications assessed.

The Case in Favour

Given the increasing likelihood of practitioners having (and being expected) to exercise discretionary powers that deeply affect the lives of others, the utmost care must be taken to ensure that they are fit to be entrusted with such power. Heavy responsibilities must not be heaped upon those who are not equipped by training or experience to bear them. On both counts, therefore, it is vital that competences should be established and from time to time re-assessed. Traditional systems of qualification cannot ensure this. There are, of course, various ways in which competence can be determined, but how it is done (and by whom) is less important than (a) that it is encouraged; (b) that the standards being applied are as consistent as possible across the country, and (c) that they are publicly recorded. This was part of the case being made for a General Council ten years ago. However, significant changes have occurred in the levels of responsibility that staff carry and in what the public expects of them.

The question of the standard of residential, day care and domiciliary care has become of increasing importance, not least because of the rapid enlargement of the private sector. The standing of those who provide care services must be improved, certainly in their own interests but, more crucially, because this affects morale which, in turn, shapes the quality of the personal care that is offered. I believe that a narrowly conceived General Council that only deals with qualified social workers would have the effect of depressing the status of the large number of personal social services staff who were thereby excluded. This would be to the detriment of many users.

The private sector, most notably in residential care, has grown dramatically in the last decade. The government is now placing requirements on local authorities that will encourage further growth, especially in the domiciliary field. The question of how the private sector is to be regulated has already become an issue of considerable significance. It seems likely that sooner or later the regulation of staffing in private services (both in terms of number and competences) will be called for, not only as a condition of registration but of the placement of local authority contracts along the lines suggested in the government's latest white paper.[1] Who is to implement and monitor such regulatory controls remains unclear; but whoever carries the responsibility will need to be able to identify the categories of staff whose competences are specified. A national registration system, such as a General Council would operate, could provide a basis upon which this could be done.

The 1980s have witnessed a new consciousness of consumer interests. It is apparent in many settings, and although it was clearly recognised in the case of the personal social services by the Barclay committee, and earlier by Seebohm, its application to that field has only slowly been realised. Despite the development of opportunities for complaint about the quality of the personal social services, there remain notable deficiencies. The brief of the national (albeit regionally-based) Ombudsman system for local government remains restricted by the 'maladministration' condition. Local systems for complaint do exist but they are unevenly spread, vary in their procedures, and deal with both serious and less serious cases. Their development is indispensable to the cause of 'consumerism'; it is right that most complaints should be dealt with locally and inexpensively. However, if the complaint is upheld and is serious, local authorities, or indeed other local organisations, can only act in ways that have local consequences. The argument for there to be a national body that is able to investigate allegations of serious professional incompetence or misconduct has been strengthened rather than weakened by the growth and improvement of other complaint systems during the 1980s. They have exposed the gaps that remain to be filled. Furthermore, a national body that has responsibility for maintaining a register of competent practitioners would have to exercise the right to remove from its list those who were judged to be unfit. In all justice this could hardly be done without there also being a national system for hearing complaints (however referred) and of conducting disciplinary proceedings.

Every tragedy that occurs within the realm of the personal social services now seems to call for a detailed inquiry. They take different forms, are conducted by different groups, report to different authorities and have variable consequences — some are official, others unofficial. Sometimes an independent panel is appointed and sometimes not. Whatever their constitution they have to be convened afresh each time, and may take little account of what similar inquiries have done or concluded. They are often expensive. There is an increasingly strong case for there to be an independent national body which would bring coherence to the present conduct of such matters. A General Council could fulfil such a function.

These are some of the important considerations that bear on the desirability of a General Council. There are also those connected with its feasibility. A General Social Work Council has become much more feasible as we approach a fully-qualified staff in field social work. By comparison with the 1960s that represents a dramatic change.

The introduction of the NVQ linked with the reform of education and training in social work and social care provides a means whereby the skills, training and experience of the unqualified will be able to be assessed and the result related to an agreed level of performance. Whatever the reservations (and there are many) about how reliable such a system will be, it is a development of the utmost importance that should be capable of refinement. In particular, it makes it more feasible to contemplate a General Social Services Council that would be able to offer registration to a substantial proportion of previously unqualified but competent care staff. The value of these developments will be enhanced by the introduction of a more flexible system of training designed to create a career structure open to all kinds of staff in the personal social services and in related fields.

The Case Against

The fact that certain changes have strengthened the case for a General Council, and especially for a General Social Services Council, is not a conclusive argument for its creation. What, over the same period, has happened to the contrary case?

There is still an issue about the respective jurisdictions of a General Council and of employers in matters of discipline, especially with respect to the local authorities. Only one thing has happened since 1982 to change the situation: the structure of employment has become more diverse, thereby creating more employers, most of whom are not democratically accountable. This trend is likely to become more pronounced when the government's proposals in its community care white paper begin to take effect.[2] Although the private and voluntary organisations with which local authorities contract to provide services will be responsible to them for what they do or do not do, individual members of their staff will answer only to their immediate employers. That will be a new problem.

However, the question of the relationship between a General Council and the local authorities as employers of social workers would remain to be settled. The local authority associations and the unions appear to view it as as much of a problem now as they considered it to be at the time for the Barclay Report. Yet it has not proved to be insurmountable in the case of other professions. Architects, solicitors, barristers, accountants, engineers and quantity surveyors are all employed in local government in substantial numbers. Would the position of social workers and social care staff, subject to a similar system of registration and regulation as these other professions, be so different? Again, there is no strong evidence that there are frequent or insuperable problems in the relationship between the NHS and the bodies responsible for doctors, nurses or the professions supplementary to medicine.

Even so, as we have seen, the demarcation of the disciplinary functions of public employers and the professional bodies is a debatable matter. It needs to be made as clear as possible where the dividing line is, even though there will continue to be grey areas.

A professional employed by a local authority is in a contractual relationship to carry out certain work, under certain conditions and in line with general policies and procedural instructions. There is also the expectation that a person engaged as a professional will be competent and conduct themselves according to prevailing professional standards. It is likely, therefore, that someone charged before a General Council would also have to face an employer's disciplinary procedures. On the other hand, by no means all employer disciplinary procedures concern matters that amount of professional incompetence or misconduct. It is obvious that most complaints against a professional will be dealt with locally by employers, since most will not be matters of serious professional shortcomings. The concept of serious professional incompetence or misconduct can be used (albeit with the aid of suitable guidelines) to delineate what a General Council would be concerned with in carrying out its disciplinary function.

Such a conclusion does not seem to be at odds with experience in other fields or with common sense. It is reasonable to expect a professional to be accountable both to an employer and to the profession of which he or she is a member and via both to the public they serve.

As well as the question of respective jurisdictions, there is also the continuing fear that a General Council, in exercising its disciplinary powers, would accentuate the problem of scapegoating. If that criticism is to be met, the disciplinary procedures of a General Council would have to be designed in ways which obliged it to take into account the full circumstances of any case and which ensured that corporate or management culpability was not allowed to pass as practitioner culpability. The critics may remain sceptical about the likelihood of that happening, and, if they are right, the opportunity for scapegoating that a General Council might create remains a significant objection. However, as suggested earlier, there is a good possibility that an independent national council, properly constituted, could protect practitioners from local scapegoating and in doing so act as a public interest trigger rather as the Audit Commission, inspection, or the House of Commons Social Services Committee might.

Finally, the claim that a General Council would be largely

irrelevant to the main problems in the personal social services also continues to have some force, not least because, during the 1980s, these problems became more numerous and more deep-rooted. However, no single body is likely to be able to wield the kind of power and influence that would make a significant impact: alliances are necessary. The question is really whether a General Council, together with other institutions working towards the same general goals, can help to achieve a higher quality of personal social services. The answer depends, therefore, upon the view that one takes of the prospects of such a fusion. For example, a General Council that incorporated the present functions of CCETSW would seem likely to be more relevant to the main problems of the personal social services than one that did not. Similarly, a Council that worked closely with the relevant research community, and with particular bodies such as the National Institute for Social Work, would be in a stronger position to exercise influence than one without such associations.

Conclusion

In my view the case for the creation of a General Social Services Council, but not merely a Social Work Council, has been strengthened by the events and trends of the 1980s. By contrast, the main case against such a body remains much as it was, albeit some of the objections, for example the exclusion of most care staff, can be met by the establishment of a body with less restrictive conditions of registration than the early models implied. There are, therefore, I conclude, stronger grounds now than before for a General Social Services Council that would include the present functions of CCETSW; but that case has to be tested further by considering the particular constitution of a General Council. That is done in the next section of the report.

Part 3

FUNCTIONS, PROCEDURES AND STRUCTURE

This part examines some of the main issues that would arise in specifying the powers, constitution and procedures of a General Social Services Council.

Chapter 15

REGISTRATION

The question of who should be registered by a General Social Services Council is a complicated matter. It would not be enough for it to set a standard of competence for registration at the barest minimum. If the Council is to serve the public interest, as all agree it should, then it has to have higher standards than that. Furthermore, it would be necessary for the standard to be reviewed from time to time as part of the active pursuit of improvement. Competence is not a fixed commodity.

However, the requirements for registration will vary according to categories of staff and types of skill. As in the nursing, midwifery and health visiting field it will be necessary for there to be more than one register, reflecting the diversity of jobs and levels of qualification in the personal social services. The UKCC holds a single professional register which is divided into 15 separate sections, indicating the kind and level of training the registered person has received and the area of practice for which they are prepared.[1] A General Social Services Council would almost certainly need to create separate parts of a register for care staff and for social workers and further divisions could be added for practice teachers, managers and so on. Other sections might be needed for approved social workers in the mental health field; for probation officers or for *guardians ad litem*. Individuals could be included in more than one section, and it would also be important for their possession of particular specialised skills or post-qualifying training to be noted. The use of particular titles associated with these divisions of the register would have to be restricted to those who were registered and in that sense registration would be mandatory. Eligibility for entry to the register would need to be established. This could be based solely upon relevant qualification. In the case of social workers that would be the new DipSW and for social care staff the possession of the impending qualification based upon a particular level of the NVQ. Qualifications alone, however, could not be taken as sufficient evidence of competence, although for the NVQ-linked awards there are grounds for taking that view.

In other professions it is common for there to be a pre-registration period after the award of a qualification during which competence is confirmed. The justification for such a probationary period is two-fold. First, whereas the processes of qualification should establish that an individual *can* undertake certain work satisfactorily, it does not ensure that they *will*. Secondly, it does not necessarily ensure that the work is performed in a professional manner. For these things to be confirmed, it is argued, a period of supervised and assessed practice is required. However, it must be noted that NALGO opposes the idea of probationary periods in principle and is sceptical whether, in practice, sufficient resources are available to ensure the level of support and supervision that the system demands.[2]

The problem of adequate supervision during any pre-registration period cannot be discounted. Certainly there is a view that this has been a stumbling block in probation (where such a system already exists), and Merrison identified it as one of the major deficiencies in medical registration. Subsequent reforms in medical education have endeavoured to meet the criticisms but problems still exist, most notably what the Merrison committee described as the pre-registration graduate being

> treated as a much needed extra pair of hands rather than as a probationer doctor still requiring supervision and training at a significant point in his career. Some young doctors find themselves burdened with responsibilities they are not yet in a position to assume; others are given duties not necessarily relevant to their training needs.[3]

A pre-registration requirement in social care and social work must strive to avoid these pitfalls, pitfalls which are all the more likely to threaten in conditions of shortage and pressure. A probationary period must be more than an enforced wait before admission to a register; otherwise it is of no value to the practitioner or the employer and, most importantly, adds nothing to the protection of the public.

The organisation and provision of good pre-registration supervision does present a problem, especially as it comes to be extended to private and voluntary settings. There is already a shortage of supervisors for student placements, and more would be needed if many social care staff are brought within the system of registration. However, two current developments are encouraging. First, the training and accreditation of practice teachers which began in 1989 will, over the next five years, produce a large number of practitioners skilled in supervision and assessment.[4] Secondly, on an even larger scale, NVQ assessments will have to be done in the main by work-based supervisors subject to some form of moderating machinery in order to ensure consistent standards. Alongside these developments it may also be possible to introduce forms of group supervision.

If there is to be a pre-registration period, which in principle appears to be desirable on several counts, its duration has to be settled. BASW[5] and ADSS[6] have suggested two years and certainly in terms of the resources that would be needed it would seem unwise to specify anything longer.

The introduction of registration poses other issues that arise from the scale of what is involved. We have already referred to the difficulty of deciding who is to be dealt with first in the programme of NVQ assessment. Likewise, if there is to be a period of pre-registration, most of the existing staff who are already qualified will have to be exempt from such a requirement: they will need to be registered through a system of blanketing-in, possibly for the first five years of the scheme.

Despite its obvious threat to standards, blanketing-in can be made conditional in ways that offer some safeguards against that happening. There could be a condition of, say, at least two years' employment in a relevant post or posts; a requirement that within a specified time certain training was undertaken or that other conditions were fulfilled before the initial registration was confirmed. However, any blanketing-in would also have to consider the position of such people as managers and teachers who are not currently practising.

Once a scheme of registration was established it would be necessary to consider the question of periodic reassessment. The confirmation of competence at one point in a person's career is no guarantee that they will continue to be competent and keep abreast of professional knowledge and developments. However, it has to be acknowledged that the reassessment of all those on the register, whatever the interval, would be a heavy task and therefore susceptible to superficiality.

Nonetheless, it should be noted that the UKCC has recently introduced periodic registration and is now considering how this can be linked to evidence of continuing competence.[7] It is unlikely that, at the outset, a General Social Services Council could implement such a scheme. Indeed, it would be foolish to assume that it could begin work on day one as a fully-fledged operation: but there should be a plan as to how such things as reassessment would develop, with target dates for their introduction. However, some aspects of a registration scheme will need to be in place from the very start, notably a means whereby those who are refused registration can appeal against the decision.[8]

Likewise, a crucial part of professional registration must be the undertaking given by those who are admitted to abide by certain codes of conduct, especially a code of ethics. The criticism that codes of ethics are inevitably rather abstract (for instance the injunction in the BASW code to recognise the value and dignity of every human being)[9] does not detract from their importance, for they are intended to express values which, although their precise interpretation may be a matter of debate, leave little doubt about what is expected.[10] Furthermore, one primary code of ethics can be supplemented by additional codes that deal with the application of principles to particular dilemmas or particular circumstances; for example, on matters of confidentiality.[11] Beyond that lies the field of guidelines which are more specifically related to practice procedures; for example, in connection with child abuse inquiries or the care of people suffering from AIDS.

In all these matters, as BASW has pointed out, a General Council would not have to start from scratch.[12] Rather good codes already exist, both within social work and elsewhere. In medicine, for example, there is the BMA's comprehensive *Philosophy and Practice of Medical Ethics*[13] and the UKCC's *Code of Professional Conduct*.[14]

A General Council would have to adopt a primary code of conduct to which all whom it admitted to the register would agree to be committed. It is unlikely that that would be different for the different sections or divisions. Indeed, were there variations, the value of its general and national applicability would be reduced. However, supplementary codes that were more specifically related to particular kinds of work, and which would probably have the status of advisory documents, might be appropriate.

There remains, of course, the issue of mandatory registration that was touched upon at the beginning of this chapter. Without it the purposes of registration are largely defeated; but it can only be imposed if either certain posts or occupations are only allowed to be held by a registered practitioner (the stronger version) or if it is made illegal for anyone but a registered person to use the registered title (the weaker version). Both restrictions could apply. This will be a key issue for negotiation. Mandatory registration has considerable implications for the structure of employment and recruitment, and with a growing private sector the range of interests is becoming increasingly wide.

Which jobs should only be open to a registered practitioner? For example, should probation officers be obliged to seek registration? There is a history of opposition to the idea. Should the post of head of a private residential home have to be filled by a registered person as a condition of the registration of the *home*? What happens about those who currently occupy posts that will be classified as only open to registered practitioners who are not and do not become eligible for registration? Problems of phasing-in will arise yet again.

A certain amount of experience of these matters has been gained from the introduction of approved social workers in mental health and from the admission of *guardians ad litem* to the local panels. But the former development, in particular, demonstrates the sensitivity of the issue and the more sub-categories of registration that are available to be linked with specific posts the more concern there is likely to be. Constructive negotiation will be at a premium.

Chapter 16

DISCIPLINE

The corollary to a General Council's power to register is the power to de-register. To do this it would have to establish a disciplinary procedure. As we have seen, both the very existence of such a function as well as its detail have been matters of considerable difference of opinion, even though the number of disciplinary actions that led to removal from the register would be likely to be minuscule by comparison with the number of registered practitioners. For those who are opposed to a General Council exercising any disciplinary powers, the details of how those powers might be implemented are irrelevant. However, some who are dubious about the matter may have their doubts dispelled (or, indeed, confirmed) once they know how a Council would be likely to discharge such responsibilities.

It is impossible in a report such as this to produce a detailed blueprint; it would also be inappropriate. But some of the issues must be highlighted and certain general principles identified, There are three cardinal issues: the processing of complaints; the investigation of complaints and the hearing of complaints.

Both the GMC and the UKCC receive a large number of complaints about professional conduct from a variety of sources. However, whereas the GMC invokes its disciplinary procedures only when a *prima facie* case of serious professional misconduct is established, the UKCC does not limit its jurisdiction to serious matters alone. That makes a difference to the pattern of complaints. So too does the source of referrals. In 1987 the GMC received 73 per cent of its complaints from the public; 6 per cent from the police (as doctors convicted of an offence are automatically referred); 18 per cent from other doctors and 4 per cent from the NHS.[1]

Clearly, complaints from the public are important and any procedure that was adopted for a General Social Services Council would have to make sure that there were no impediments to such complaints being made. Likewise, as with medicine, nursing and the professions supplementary to medicine, it would seem essential that practitioners who were convicted of an offence were referred, although trivial or minor offences might be excluded. Such a provision could be related to the new arrangements for the disclosure of the criminal background of those with access to children.[2] Some referrals would be made by local authorities or other organisations with their own complaints and disciplinary procedures. It would be crucial for it to be agreed when that should happen.

These matters are important in principle but also because the manner in which they are resolved in practice will influence the volume of complaints that will have to be dealt with by a General Council and that, in its turn, will affect the choice of procedures. Whatever their volume may be, however, it will be necessary for there to be a means of screening them in order to establish which are inappropriate (for example, which should be referred to the local authority or to the Ombudsman); which can be dealt with informally and which, *prima facie,* demand a further investigation with the possibility that disciplinary action will be invoked. The GMC, for example, has a four-tier screen. Complaints are first seen by the Council's staff and

> most are passed swiftly to the preliminary screener — a senior member of Council, often the President — who concludes many of the complaints. . . . Those that are the result of convictions or that raise in the mind of the preliminary screener a question of serious professional misconduct are referred to the preliminary proceedings committee. The committee concludes many cases but refers to the professional misconduct committee cases that may well be of serious professional misconduct.[3]

There is a similar system in nursing, midwifery and health visiting and for the professions supplementary to medicine.

However, the way in which the screening is managed is of the utmost importance and at least four principles should guide which is chosen for a General Social Services Council. First, the initial screening should not be undertaken by a single person and should have lay involvement. Secondly, where complainants are referred to another more appropriate system a full explanation should be offered and any necessary help provided to enable them to transfer their complaint, plus an opportunity to appeal against the transfer. The prior agreement of the agency to which it is intended that a complaint be transferred should be secured. Thirdly, if steps are taken at this stage to resolve the matter informally, the complainants should be clear what the alternatives are and then agree to the informal approach, but without prejudice to resort to formal proceedings if these should fail. Finally, if the complaint is to be referred onwards and upwards the complainant should be offered any necessary help in organising the next stage in the presentation of their case. As Smith has pointed out in his profile of the GMC, the preliminary screener is 'a powerful gatekeeper',[4] although in future a lay member will be included in the procedure for initial consideration. The public certainly needs to be reassured that they are not being fobbed off at this stage by a professional interest group anxious to protect its reputation and its members. The possibility that that impression will be given is real. For instance, few complaints passing through the GMC's preliminary screen have been from the public, 'apart from "sex" or "confidentiality" cases',[5] despite their overwhelming preponderance amongst the initial referrals.

If a complaint passes the preliminary screen it is necessary to consider the next stages. The GMC has a preliminary proceedings committee that considers the evidence provided by the complainant, the response of the doctor in question, as well as the results of any investigations that its own staff may have conducted.[6] The issue is considered on paper. About half the cases in any year originate from convictions. The preliminary screener is present as well as a legal assessor. There is a lay member. The committee may issue a letter of advice or admonition (45 per cent in 1988); refer the case to the health committee (13 per cent); take no further action (7 per cent), or pass the matter to the full professional conduct committee (31 per cent). A few cases stand adjourned.

Again, the details are less important than the issues they reflect and the questions of principle that they raise. The more steps that there are in the screening process the greater care will need to be taken that justice is not only being done but is seen to be done. Yet, given the potential volume of complaints *some* filtering system is essential or the procedure will be overwhelmed.

That is in nobody's interest since one of the principles of a complaints or disciplinary procedure should be that matters are dealt with expeditiously and that the parties are not kept waiting throughout seemingly interminable delays. That can easily happen. The UKCC is concerned that in 1987-8 'there continued to be a disturbingly large backlog of cases waiting to be heard by its Professional Conduct Committee'.[7] The fact that the UKCC inherited such a backlog should be borne in mind in the case of a General Social Services Council, were complaints that were made during the period of its establishment held over for its consideration when it became operational.

There is clearly a tension: a screening system is essential but is liable to be seen as untrustworthy by complainants. In these circumstances it is of the utmost importance that as many complaints as possible are dealt with locally and informally; but for that to be done satisfactorily and fairly there must be local procedures in which both the public and the professionals have confidence. Paradoxically, therefore, the improvement of local complaints procedures is a *sine qua non* for the successful operation of a national professional disciplinary system. Dissatisfaction with local arrangements is likely to result in an impossibly large and probably inappropriate wave of complaints being directed to a General Council.

There is an important issue with respect to practitioners whose unsatisfactory behaviour is considered to be attributable to sickness, drug addiction or alcoholism. They obviously need to be treated differently, though still with the possibility that they can be prevented from practising. In principle the problem of sick practitioners should be dealt with locally, early and as informally as possible, perhaps with the help of something similar to the National Counselling Service for Sick Doctors that has been set up by the Royal Colleges and the BMA.[8] Better 'sickness procedures' need to be implemented locally and a General Council could provide a lead in the matter. That notwithstanding, it will need to fashion its own procedures to take account of the fact that some practitioners against whom allegations are made will be sick. How, by whom and when that is determined will also have to be settled. Even so, a Council would also certainly need to establish a 'health' committee, similar perhaps to those which exist in the GMC and the UKCC. In both these cases the arrangements are generally agreed to work well.

If, after all the preliminaries, a case reaches a formal hearing there is the possibility that the practitioner involved may lose the right to practise and hence his or her principal livelihood. It will be necessary, therefore, for the proceedings to be conducted according to due process and for them to observe the tenets of natural justice. The membership of the committee will almost certainly have to be drawn from the Council as a whole and should reflect its compostion; in particular there should not be an overwhelming professional representation. There is also the question of the selection of a chairperson. In my view, as with chairpersons of tribunals, they should be specially trained or legally qualified. It is crucial that the conduct of such hearings is above reproach. There are questions about who presents the case against the practitioner — the Council through its solicitor or the complainant (again, probably through their solicitor or counsel); about the nature of admissable evidence; about how decisions of guilt or innocence are reached; about assistance with the parties' legal expenses and about the balance between adversarial or inquisitorial approaches. All these issues will have to be sorted out, perhaps with the advice of the Council on Tribunals, even though a disciplinary committee would be considered to be a domestic tribunal and fall outside its jurisdiction. BASW's disciplinary procedures (although so far rarely used) may also provide useful guidelines, especially in defining 'professional misconduct'.[9]

If a practitioner is found guilty of the charge by a full disciplinary committee (it might be called a Professional Conduct Committee as in medicine and nursing) it will have to decide what penalty to impose. Typically these range from removal from the register, through suspension, to continued registration being made conditional upon certain requirements being met. There are conflicting principles here too. The complainant will probably seek punishment whereas the council may favour a policy of rehabilitation, especially if it is dealing with cases of incompetence that involve no misconduct. Should rehabilitation be chosen as the preferred course of action, it would be essential that the complainant be informed about the outcome.

Whatever the sentence there will have to be provision for appeal, almost certainly to the judicial committee of the Privy Council. Likewise, there will probably have to be provision for practitioners who have been removed from the register to reapply for admission after a set period.

Chapter 17

STATUS, CONSTITUTION, STRUCTURE AND FUNDING

Matters of registration and discipline, of course, have to be set within the constitutional status of any General Council. First, given the powers that it would exercise it will be essential that it is created by Statute. BASW prepared a draft bill in 1979[1] which would provide a useful starting point for current discussion. There is also other comparable legislation, most notably for doctors, nurses and the professions supplementary to medicine. However, these can only be guidelines: they should not be adopted uncritically.

The main issue is the constitution and composition of the Council itself. Much of the public criticism of professional regulative bodies has centred upon the heavy preponderance of professional control. Professions, and indeed other occupations, are not readily trusted to regulate and discipline themselves without regard to their own interests and domestic loyalties. It is crucial, therefore, that an appropriate range of interests is represented in the Council's membership and that the same broad range is reflected in its principal committees. The problem arises, however, in deciding what those 'proper' interests are and how those who represent them are to be selected. The first schedule to BASW's draft bill, for example, identified 32 interests that they considered should be represented, some by more than one person, giving a minimum of 48 members plus a chairperson. The GMC has almost 100 members but the UKCC only 45. CCETSW has 25. Size matters. In my view the Council should be as small as possible — more like 25 than 100 — commensurate with adequate representation. The key interests that should be represented are those of the profession; the consumers; the employers; the employees (as distinct from professional interests); education and training and government. It will be necessary to consider how particular interests within the consumer group will be reflected; for example, the interests of women and ethnic minorities. At a second level of specificity Scottish, Welsh and Northern Ireland interests would be included plus the sub-categories that exist within the profession, amongst the consumers, the employers and employees. In my view BASW's draft schedule included too many representatives of the sub-categories and was flawed by the omission of the consumer voice, although it has since insisted that it must be heard.

The exact size and composition of the Council will in part depend upon the structure of the organisation as a whole. If, as is generally suggested, it incorporates the present functions of CCETSW then there will have to be an education and training committee; there will need to be another that oversees matters of registration and another that deals with disciplinary affairs. There may need to be others; for example, those concerned with research or with inquiries that go beyond the investigation of allegations against individuals. The Council itself should be strictly concerned with issues of policy and strategic planning. Some members of the Council would have to serve on each of the principal committees, but it would seem sensible were there to be a measure of additional recruitment to their membership. This could be used to reflect a wider range of more specific interests. Not everyone on the Council should serve on all committees and not everyone on the committees need necessarily be a member of Council.

The question of chairpersons is, as I have already suggested, of considerable importance. General practice in this matter suggests that the first chair of the Council should be appointed by the Secretary of State (although after consultation) and that thereafter they should be elected by the Council. However, there is a strong case for the post of chairperson to the Council to be paid, and to demand more than occasional involvement, albeit for a fixed term. Not only would that be a recognition of the importance of the Council but also a means by which agreed policy could be firmly steered.

How should the members of the Council be selected once the interests to be represented have been decided? It will, I believe, have to be done indirectly, either through elections or nomination depending upon the manner in which the interests are organised.

There is an argument, however, that at least those who represent the professional interest should be elected by the registered membership. In theory that seems an attractive idea; in practice it does not. First, because (as the UKCC experience has illustrated) such elections are difficult and costly to arrange (the last UKCC election to national boards cost some £315,000); and secondly, because there is unlikely to be any local, or even regional, organisation of registered practitioners that can select candidates; thirdly, under these circumstances the candidates would be unknown to the vast majority of the electors and, finally, their accountability to that electorate would be difficult, if not impossible, to ensure.

The same principle of indirect selection via representative organisations will probably have to apply to the committees, although it might also be desirable to enable them to exercise a power of co-option. The chair of these committees will also bear a rather heavy cluster of responsibilities and, as with the chairperson of the Council, it may be wise to press for them to be paid. They would have to be granted ex-officio membership of the Council. The selection of these chairpersons, however, should be left to the Council.

It would be impossible for the Council to discharge all its responsibilities from a central administration. The present regional structure of CCETSW may offer a useful model, particularly for the Council's education and training functions. Whether that model, or one like it, should also be adopted for other functions — such as discipline or research — is another matter: I suspect not. In principle, however, it seems right that as much of the Council's work as can be done efficiently at a regional level should be located there. However, it is widely agreed that the UKCC model of separate national boards for educational and training functions has created difficulties and that a General Social Services Council should not follow in that direction.

There is need for a broad policy, codes and standards to be nationally decided and applied. Nevertheless, it has to be recognised that the situations in Scotland, Wales and Northern Ireland are different from those in England. There is, for example, the need for a Council to deal directly with the Scottish and Welsh officers on some matters and with other bodies that have national identities. Likewise NCVQ's jurisdiction does not extend to Scotland although its counterpart, SCOVTEC, has established a care sector liaison group. Similarly, as the government's community care white paper[2] implicitly recognises, the less extensive private sector of welfare in Scotland and Northern Ireland casts the public authorities there in a much more central role. Political, administrative and cultural differences need to be considered alongside the need for a country-wide system for the preservation and promotion of good standards. The problem of reconciling these objectives might be met by the creation (or continuation in a modified form) of national committees along the lines that CCETSW has established.[3] These were originally solely advisory but since 1989 they have also exercised a degree of executive responsibility, particularly in Scotland.

Some recognition of the particular statuses of Scotland, Wales and Northern Ireland will be essential if a single national body is to be created that pursues United Kingdom-wide policies and procedures. The form of that recognition may need to vary as between the three countries. In Scotland especially the personal social services operate within a different legal and administrative structure that requires to be taken into account.

Finally, there is the question of how a General Social Services Council might be financed. There are two fundamental considerations. First, its work will have to be adequately funded but secondly, there is the need to preserve its independence from government or, indeed, from any other single sponsoring body. A solution might be found in the pattern that prevails in the UKCC. Following an initial subsidy, the UKCC is now virtually self-financing through its registration fee system and therefore financially independent.[4] It is likely that the similar functions that a General Social Services Council would perform would have to be subsidised for an initial period until the volume of registration built up and the start-up costs had been met. However, some functions as well as education and training (for example, the conduct of expensive general inquiries) would continue to need to be publicly funded, whether directly or indirectly.

Even so, the question of fee income is far from straightforward.

Although a registration fee will have to be compulsory, its

level and how often it will need to be renewed raise some difficulties. The amount has to bear some relationship to salary levels and it has to be a sum that practitioners are actually willing to pay. The doctors' revolt against the GMC's fee (that led to the setting-up of the Merrison committee) is well known. If there is to be a once-for-all fee it will have to be large. It would seem preferable for it to be fixed at a lower level but made periodically renewable. The UKCC has recently moved to a triennial formula.

Should the Council's 'independent' income be drawn only from individual registration fees or should employers also be asked to pay a levy, perhaps in relation to the number of registered staff they employ? There is a partial precedent in the registration fee required of private residential homes. An employer fee would not necessarily have to be large; but it would acknowledge that employers gained certain benefits from the registration system — although there will doubtless be those who deny it.

If a General Council's responsibilities come to extend beyond the areas of education and training, registration and discipline (for example to research or to the conduct of inquiries), then there are likely to be further sources of income. On the other hand, no doubt the Council will also wish to commission certain work to be done, for example in drawing up codes of practice or guidelines. Some of this work will have to be paid for.

It is impossible in this report to review the financial issues surrounding the establishment of a General Social Services Council in anything like the detail needed. But the experience of CCETSW is available as well as that of other bodies like the UKCC. In the year ending March 1988, for example, the UKCC's income from fees of all kinds amounted to £4.2m although in the previous year, before periodic registration it was £2.4m — a sum that fell considerably short of expenditure. The initial registration fee is now £10 plus £30 for each triennial payment. Extra entries in the register, for example to show that a particular course has been completed, cost £15 and admission to an additional division of the register £14. The professions supplementary to medicine charge an initial fee of £11 plus £7.30 per annum thereafter. They make no charge for registering additional qualifications. Thus, a fee of between £10 and £15 seems to be indicated: not, I would suggest, a prohibitive figure. An average fee income of £15 per person would produce £1m per 67,000 registered practitioners.

However, it is important to emphasise that the education and training responsibilities of a Council that incorporated the present activities of CCETSW would continue to need to be financed from public sources. Fee income could only properly be expected to cover registration and its associated functions.

Chapter 18

SCOPE

Those who advocated the establishment of a General Social Services Council, rather than simply a General Social Work Council, have been anxious that social care staff should have the opportunity to be registered; but they have also argued that the role of such a body should be more broadly conceived. Since the early 1980s this view has gained increasing support. Indeed, as was pointed out in Chapter 2, some consider that a General Council would only be fully justified if it acted as the champion of the personal social services and of those who use or need them. In this view, it should generate a continual and concerted pressure for the preservation and improvement of standards, acting as a watchdog, advocate, source of information and advice.

These are attractive notions but they tend to ignore the political complexities that would confront a body that assumed these functions as well as regulative responsibilities. The personal social services contain an assortment of interests, not all of which are compatible. Federations of interests are notoriously difficult to engineer and maintain. The fate of the Personal Social Services Council is a case in point. It is hazardous to construct bodies that will be expected to assume over-arching responsibilities from the outset — and be judged accordingly.

None of this is to say that a General Social Services Council should not aspire to such a role; only that it is necessary to acknowledge its primary role and not impose other undue burdens at the start, few of which are likely to be fulfilled satisfactorily. In my view the core function of the Council is the regulation of the profession. That must be its point of departure.

Once established, however, it will be essential for the Council to become involved in associated activities, but these should evolve rather than be constitutionally prescribed. There are several such activities that will call for early attention.

A Council that is concerned with the promotion of high standards of practice will need to be engaged in a continuous programme (whether directly or indirectly) that enables these to be imaginatively codified, regularly monitored and continuously refined. In doing so the articulation of principles and values will be of the utmost importance; for example, in exploring how best the users of services can be involved in the evaluation of practitioner competence; what scope there is for peer review; how group performance might best be assessed or what management arrangements facilitate good practice. In exploring such matters the Council needs to make sure that there is a constant flow of ideas back and forth between education and training and practice. This kind of development work will be essential if the Council is to serve the public interest by engaging *actively* in the promotion of high standards rather than resting content to ensure an adequate minimum that avoids the worst scandals or public outcries. If this is to be done, constructive working relationships — consultative, collaborative and chivvying — will have to be forged with a wide range of groups and organisations. A 'development' arm will almost certainly be necessary.

The Council should also be a source of reliable information about the areas of its responsibilities; one hesitates to say about the personal social services, for this would be a daunting undertaking, at least in the early years. Yet even to meet the somewhat narrower requirement for the provision of good information it would have to undertake, or encourage others to undertake, the development of better data bases (for example, with respect to workforce characteristics); the collection and organisation of presently scattered and unstandardised information; and the systematic analysis of its own experience (for instance, with respect to what the complaints it receives indicate about wider pressures and problems). It may wish to carry out (or sponsor) some research itself but, at least at the beginning, the first priority would lie in the gathering, analysis and presentation of 'intelligence'. Even that will not be able to be done single-handed; the collaboration of other bodies will be crucial.

Some have argued that a General Council should become involved in the evaluation of services. That would be a major responsibility. In my view, it would be more appropriate for it to approach the issue from the perspective of development. There are exacting problems, still largely unresolved, about how services are best evaluated, by whom and with what consequences. It is essential that the exploration of such matters is kept going, and at a high level. That would be the kind of thing for which the Council should take an active responsibility: setting the agenda, pressing for action and checking on what transpires.

As we have seen, there is also a good deal of support for the idea that a General Council should offer an independent inquiry service based upon a standing group. Various organisations may wish to take advantage of such a facility. We have already touched upon some of its advantages, but it could also make a valuable contribution to the Council's intelligence-gathering function. The experience of conducting numerous inquiries would begin to build a basis for generalisation (or discerning the patterns and regularities), although for that to happen it would have to be made a conscious objective. On this and the other grounds that have been mentioned, therefore, a strong case can be made for the Council to provide an independent inquiry service.

These are suggestions for the kinds of ways in which the extended functions of a Council might be developed. Others could certainly be added; but in my view the temptation to take on too much too early should be resisted. Extended functions will be best built upon a foundation of trust, confidence, experience and a paramount concern for the promotion of the best possible standards of service. That being so, one of the crucial questions is: how best is the performance of the Council itself to be monitored? That should come high on the agenda.

Part 4
THE ESSENTIAL CONCLUSIONS

This presents the skeleton of the conclusions.

Chapter 19

CONCLUSIONS

There are five essential conclusions that I draw from this review:

1. There are respectable arguments both in favour and against the establishment of an independent body to regulate and promote good practice in social work and social care.
2. However, the case for such a body has been strengthened by a variety of events since the Barclay report judged it to be unproven in 1982. By contrast the case against it has remained much as it was.
3. In particular, the case for a General Social Services Council rather than a Social Work Council has become more compelling. I believe its establishment is justified when that justification is tested against the criterion of what serves the public interest.
4. To be fully effective the work of a General Council should be closely associated with the present responsibilities of the Central Council for Education and Training in Social Work.
5. The refinement and implementation of these proposals will call for further work well beyond the scope of this report. There are many practical problems to be resolved, and some of those upon whose collaboration the scheme's success would partly depend may remain opposed to certain aspects. A period of detailed negotiation and planning will be required and, to that end, appropriate machinery will need to be created and a time-scale for moving forward set.

NOTES AND REFERENCES

Chapter 1
Background

1. See, the Association of Social Workers, *A Report on the Registration of the Social Worker* (Cormack), 1954.
2. *Report of the Committee of Inquiry into the Care and Supervision Provided in Relation to Maria Colwell*, HMSO, 1974.
3. *Accreditation in Social Work: a Second and Final Report*, a report of the Joint Steering Group operating under the auspices of the Association of Directors of Social Services, the Association of Directors of Social Work, the British Association of Social Workers, the Conference of Chief Probation Officers and the Residential Care Association, 1980.
4. M. Malherbe, *Accreditation in Social Work: Principles and Issues in Context: A Contribution to the Debate,* CCETSW, Study 4, 1980.
5. *Ibid*, p. 121.
6. *Social Workers: Their Role and Tasks* (Barclay), NISW/Bedford Square Press, 1982; esp. ch 12.
7. For a more detailed analysis of the evidence see J. Thomas, *Responses to the Barclay Report*, National Institute for Social Work, paper no. 16, 1983; esp. ch 3.

Chapter 2
The Arguments in Favour

1. British Association of Social Workers, *The Case for a Social Work Council*, 1987; p. 1. See also D. Jones and S. Woolfe, 'Towards a New Professionalism', *Community Care*, 25 June, 1987; pp. 16-20.
2. *Report of the Committee of Inquiry into the Regulation of the Medical Profession* (Merrison), cmnd. 6018, HMSO, 1975; see ch 1 especially.
3. BASW, *A Code of Ethics for Social Work;* SCA, *Code of Practice for Social Care,* nd. The issues surrounding the BASW Code of Ethics are discussed in D. Watson (ed.), *A Code of Ethics for Social Work: The Second Step,* Routledge and Kegan Paul, 1985.
4. The Association of Directors of Social Services, *Registration and a Social Work Council? A Discussion Document Prepared for the ADSS Parliamentary Sub-Committee* (SeQuiera), 1986; p. 2.
5. *Ibid.*
6. SCA, *Horizon,* p.28, May 1987; para 4.
7. BASW, *Towards a Partnership in Practice: A Note Relevant to Motion 6,* AGM, 1983; para 10.
8. *A Child in Mind: Protection of Children in a Responsible Society: The Report of the Commission of Inquiry into the Circumstances Surrounding the Death of Kimberley Carlile,* London Borough of Greenwich, 1987; p. 35.

Chapter 3
The Problems and the Objections

1. See, *Horizon, op. cit.*
2. *Social Workers: Their Role and Tasks, op. cit.*, p. 184.
3. *Ibid.* More generally, see J. Thomas, *Responses to the Barclay Report, op. cit.*, ch 3.
4. GMC, *Report of the Working Party on the Council's Disciplinary Procedures in Response to Allegations of Failure to Provide a Good Standard of Medical Care*, 1989; p. 1.
5. *Ibid.*
6. *The Health Service: Working for Patients*, HMSO, 1989; pp. 39-40.
7. Quoted in GMC, *Working Party Report, op. cit.*, p. 8.
8. *Ibid.*, p. 9.
9. Advisory, Conciliation and Arbitration Service, Code of Practice, no. 1, *Disciplinary Practice and Procedure in Employment*, HMSO, 1988. Adoption of the code is recommended by the National Joint Council for Local Authorities' Administrative, Professional, Technical and Clerical Services in their *Scheme of Conditions of Service,* 1988; see the section on 'Official Conduct'. Furthermore, although the ACAS code is not mandatory the Employment Protection Act, 1975 (sect. 6/11) makes it clear that the failure to observe its provisions is admissable in evidence in proceedings before an industrial tribunal or the Central Arbitration Committee.
10. NALGO, *General Social Work Council — A Statement,* paper tabled at CCETSW Council meeting, July, 1987; p. 3. See also, for an elaboration, D. Reed, 'Why We Say "No,",' *Community Care,* 17 Sept., 1987; pp. 20-1.
11. United Kingdom Central Council for Nursing, Midwifery and Health Visiting, *The First Five Years, 1983-1988,* 1988; p. 18.
12. *Social Workers: Their Role and Tasks, op. cit.*, pp. 187-97.

Chapter 4
The Composition of the Workforce

1. Ministry of Health and Department of Health for Scotland, *Report of the Working Party on Social Workers in Local Authority Health and Welfare Services* (Younghusband), HMSO, 1959; p. 83.
2. Home Office, *Report on the Work of the Children's Department 1964-6,* HC 603, HMSO, 1967; p. 17.
3. *Report of the Committee on Local Authority and Allied Personal Social Services* (Seebohm), cmnd. 3703, HMSO, 1968; appendix M, part III.
4. *Ibid.*
5. Department of Health and Social Security, *Manpower and Training for the Social Services* (Birch), HMSO, 1976; pp. 154-5.
6. CCETSW, *Training for Residential Work,* 1973; pp. 8-9.
7. *Social Workers: Their Role and Tasks, op. cit.*, pp. 24-26.
8. See CCETSW, *Abstracts of Data* (various years).
9. Local Government Training Board, *Survey of Manpower and Qualifications within Social Services Departments in England and Wales and Social Work Departments in Scotland,* 1986. See also for a commentary, N. Murray, 'An Illustration of Ignorance', *Social Services Insight,* 13 Sept., 1986.
10. LGTB, *Survey of Manpower, op. cit.*, p. 35.

11. *Ibid*, p. 43.
12. *Ibid.*, p. 28.
13. DHSS, *Manpower and Training, op. cit.*, p. 43.
14. *Report of the Working Group on Workforce Planning and Training Needs in the Personal Social Services* (Webb), 1987; table 1.5. As well as drawing upon the LGTB survey the working group was able to use the results of a valuable report compiled by the Social Work Education Development Group in the North West, *Workforce Analysis*, 1987.
15. LACSAB and ADSS, *Survey of Social Services Employment, 1988*, 1988; pp. 11-13.
16. *Ibid.*, table 4.2, p. 25.
17. *Ibid.*, Annex E.
18. See for evidence of this NALGO, *Social Work in Crisis: A Study of Conditions in Six Local Authorities*, 1989. (Study undertaken by P. Hayes *et al*, Department of Social Work Studies, University of Southampton. NALGO commissioned the enquiry because it was 'concerned by the persistent scapegoating of individual social workers and wanted an examination of working conditions, staffing levels and changes in demand for services'. (Foreward))
19. (1) Subject to paragraph (2) of this Rule, a person who has not been awarded a Certificate of Qualification in Social Work by the Central Council for Education and Training in Social Work or another qualification which that Council has approved as equivalent to that Certificate shall not be appointed to be a probation officer at the rank of Probation Officer, Senior Probation Officer or Assistant Chief Probation Officer.

    (2) This Rule shall not apply to a person who, at the time when these rules come into force, has been appointed to be or is serving as a probation officer at any rank in any part of the United Kingdom or has previously served as a probation officer in Great Britain in an appointment which has been confirmed in accordance with Rule 25 of the Probation Rules 1968(a) or any corresponding provision in any Rules revoked by those Rules or has previously served as a probation officer in Northern Ireland, nor to a trainee probation officer.

Chapter 5
Inquiries and Public Confidence in Social Work

1. *Report on the Circumstances which led to the Boarding-Out of Dennis and Terence O'Neill at Bank Farm, Minsterley and Steps Taken to Supervise their Welfare*, cmd. 6636, HMSO, 1945.
2. DHSS, *Report of the Committee of Inquiry into the Care and Supervision Provided in Relation to Maria Colwell*, HMSO, 1974.
3. *A Child in Trust: The Report of the Panel of Inquiry into the Circumstances Surrounding the Death of Jasmine Beckford*, London Borough of Brent, 1985; *A Child in Mind: Protection of Children in a Responsible Society: The Report of the Commission of Inquiry into the Circumstances Surrounding the Death of Kimberley Carlile*, London Borough of Greenwich, 1985; and *Report of the Inquiry into Child Abuse in Cleveland 1987*, cmd. 412, HMSO, 1988.
4. *A Child in Trust, op. cit.*, pp. 287, 292 and 298.
5. *Ibid.*, p. 293.

6. *Ibid.*, pp. 204-5 and 304.
7. *A Child in Mind, op. cit.*, p. 217.
8. *Ibid.*, p. 35.
9. *Ibid.*, pp. 179 and 182.
10. *Report of the Inquiry into Child Abuse in Cleveland, op. cit.*
11. *Ibid.*, p. 85.
12. CCETSW, *Care for Tomorrow: the Case for Reform of Education and Training for Social Workers and other Care Staff,* 1987; para 3.1.1.
13. *Liam Johnson Review: Report of a Panel of Inquiry,* London Borough of Islington, 1989; p. 10.
14. *Ibid.*, p. 11.
15. *The Independent,* 5 Dec., 1989.
16. *The Independent,* 8 Dec., 1989.
17. Roger Clough, *Scandals in Residential Centres: A Report to the Wagner Committee,* University of Bristol, 1987.
18. *Report of the Inquiry into Nye Bevan Lodge* (Richard Clough), London Borough of Southwark, 1987.
19. *Ibid.*
20. H. Harman and M. Lowe, *No Place Like Home: a Report of the First Year's Work of the Registered Homes Tribunal,* Labour Party (Putting People First), 1986.

Chapter 6
Community Care

1. See, for example, A. Walker (ed.), *Community Care: The Family, the State and Social Policy,* Blackwell/Robertson, 1982 and, more recently, his 'Community Care' in M. McCarthy (ed.), *The New Politics of Welfare: An Agenda for the 1990s?* Macmillan, 1989.
2. For an account and explanation see R. A. Parker, *The Elderly and Residential Care: Australian Lessons for Britain,* Gower, 1987.
3. *Caring for People, op. cit.*
4. *Ibid.*, p. 21.
5. CCETSW, *Care for Tomorrow, op. cit.*, p. 9.
6. Home Office, *Supervision and Punishment in the Community: a Framework for Action,* HMSO, 1990.
7. See E. Farmer and R. A. Parker, *Trials and Tribulations* (forthcoming).
8. *Community Care: Agenda for Action: A Report to the Secretary of State for Social Services,* Sir Roy Griffiths, HMSO, 1988; p. 28.

Chapter 7
The Independent Sector

1. For a fuller discussion see R. A. Parker, *Welfare Provision for the Elderly: The Contribution of the Private Sector,* National Institute for Social Work, 1989 (to be published by HMSO as a section of the UK report forming part of the EEC's 'Age Care in Europe Project').
2. See R. A. Parker, *The Elderly and Residential Care, op. cit.*
3. DHSS, *Public Support for Residential Care; Report of a Joint Central and Local Government Working Party* (Firth), 1987.
4. *Workforce Planning and Training, op. cit.*, table 1.6.

5. Estimated from DHSS, *Health and Personal Social Services Statistics for England*, Government Statistical Service, HMSO, 1987.
6. *The Residential Care Homes Regulations*, 1984; for example, sections 10(1), 12(1)(a), 25(1) and 28(a).
7. *Caring for People, op. cit.*, p. 5.
8. *Ibid.*, p. 6.
9. Home Office, *Supervision and Punishment in the Community, op. cit.* See also the parallel white paper, Home Office, *Crime, Justice and Protecting the Public: The Government's Proposals for Legislation*, cmd. 965, HMSO, 1990.
10. Personal communication.
11. *Workforce Planning and Training, op. cit.*, table 1.5.

Chapter 8
National Vocational Qualifications

1. OPCS, *Labour Force Survey, 1984*, HMSO, 1985.
2. See, for example, *Training for Jobs*, cmd. 9135, HMSO, 1984 and *Employment — The Challenge to the Nation*, cmd. 9474, HMSO, 1986.
3. See, for example, *Education and Training for Young People*, cmd. 9482, HMSO, 1985.
4. MSC and DES, *Review of Vocational Qualifications in England and Wales* (DeVille), 1986.
5. *Ibid.*, pp. 4-5.
6. The levels of award are based on the following descriptions taken from the *Review of Vocational Qualifications, op. cit.*

   I **Basic Level**
   Occupational competence in performing a range of tasks under supervision
   They will typically include the ability to perform a minimum number of work activities, within realistic time constraints to specified standards (usually under supervision and in a restricted range of working conditions and contexts) necessary for employment in a specified group of activities.

   II **Standard Level**
   Occupational competence in performing a wider range of more demanding tasks with limited supervision
   Qualifications . . . for many occupations whose requirements are significant but which are primarily of a routine and predictable character . . . should ensure competent performance in an extended range of contexts . . . with minimum guidance and induction.

   III **Advanced Level**
   Occupational competence required for satisfactory, responsible performance in a defined occupation or range of jobs
   Qualifications at this level will be awarded for competences needed for occupations which are not of a routine character and which may require application in a variety of contexts and roles. They will indicate ability to perform a broad range of work-related activities, including many that are complex, difficult and non-routine, appropriate to sustaining regular processes and outputs, to specified standards.

The minimum standards of qualifications at this level . . . (and) the skills achieved at this level may be of such a nature as to indicate capability in supervisory and junior management roles, or to progress into advanced further education and training. Awards at this level will be appropriate for many skilled jobs and occupations.

IV **Higher Level**
Competence to design and specify defined tasks, products or processes and to accept responsibility for the work of others
. . . for occupations with specialist or supervisory or professional requirements and which need the capacity to adapt to major job rôle changes while maintaining full accountability and responsibility for personal outputs and those of others.
They will indicate ability to perform a comprehensive range of complex, difficult and often specialised work-related activities . . . and to undertake the training and the supervision of others . . . The skills achieved at this level may be sufficiently extensive to indicate capability for senior management.

V **Professional Levels**
Should reflect competence at professional level, with mastery of a range of relevant knowledge and the ability to apply it at a higher level than IV
At present the remit of the National Council does not extend to awarding qualifications above level IV.

7. *Ibid.*, p. 2.
8. *Working Together — Education and Training,* cmd. 9823, HMSO, 1986.
9. *Ibid.*, p. 17.
10. *Ibid.*, p. 24.
11. See, Care Sector Consortium Steering Group, *Residential, Domiciliary and Day Care Project: Background Material Relevant to the Preparation of Draft National Standards,* 1989; and Care Sector Consortium, *Information Pack,* 1989.
12. Care Sector Consortium Steering Group, *Residential, Domiciliary and Day Care Project: Draft National Standards for Consultation,* 1989.
13. Webb working party, *op. cit.*
14. LGTB, *A System for Workforce Analysis for Social Services Departments,* nd.
15. See, NCVQ, *Extensions of the NVQ Framework above Level IV; A Consultative Document,* 1989.
    The standards of competence suggested for the 'higher' level is as follows:
    Competence in the pursuit of a senior occupation or profession — as an employee or as a self-employed person — including the ability to apply a significant range of fundamental principles and techniques to diagnosis, planning and problem solving. Extensive knowledge and understanding will be required to underpin competence at this level, together with capability in management and supervision for executive and some professional fields (p. 6).
16. CCETSW, *Care for Tomorrow, op. cit.*
17. BASW, *Report of the Competence in Practice Working Party,* 1979. See also, in a somewhat different context, CCETSW, *Accreditation of Agencies and Practice Teachers in Social Work Education,* paper 26.1, 1987.

Chapter 9
The Reform of Education and Training
1. CCETSW, *Care for Tomorrow, op. cit.*
2. *Ibid.*, p. 25.
3. *Ibid.*, p. 5. Details of the minimum requirements expected of the social worker at the point of qualification appear in Annexe 4, p. 57.
4. *Ibid.*, p. 25.
5. For further details, see CCETSW, *Annual Report for 1987-8*, 1989.

Chapter 10
The European Dimension
1. These are: doctors, nurses, dentists, pharmacists, midwives, architects and veterinary surgeons.
2. See Council Directive 89/48/EEC in the *Official Journal of the European Communities*, 24 Jan., 1989.
3. *Ibid.*, general title.
4. For a detailed discussion of these matters and for the background see, H. Barr, *Social Work in its European Context*, CCETSW, 1989. See also, 'Watching the Directives', *Community Care*, 5 Oct., 1989.
5. *The Report from the European Directive Workshop*, CCETSW, 1988; p. 19.
6. *Ibid.*, p. 20.

Chapter 11
Social Services Inspection
1. For an account of some of the issues in the early years see, R. Klein and P. Hall, *Caring for Quality in the Caring Services: Options for Policy*, Centre for Studies in Social Policy, 1974.
2. *Social Workers: Their Role and Tasks, op. cit.*, p. 187.
3. The Social Services Inspectorate and the DHSS, *Mission Statement*, nd.; p. 2.
4. *Ibid*, p. 5.
5. Home Office, *Supervision and Punishment in the Community, op. cit.*, p. 20.
6. C. Peaker, *The Crisis in Residential Care.* NCVO, 1986.
7. *Residential Care: A Positive Choice* (Wagner), HMSO, 1988; pp. 54-6.
8. SCA and ADSS, *Towards Excellence for Residential Care. Regulating Residential Services: Formulating Guidelines for Quality Assurance and Quality Control*, 1989.
9. *Caring for People, op. cit.*, p. 6.
10. See, for example, J. Thomas, *op. cit.*, pp. 108-110.
11. *Report of the Committee on Local Government Finance* (Layfield), cmnd. 6453, HMSO, 1976.
12. Audit Commission, *Making a Reality of Community Care*, HMSO, 1986.

Chapter 12
The Local Commissioners for Administration
1. Local Government Act, HMSO, 1974; sect. 23.
2. *Committee of Inquiry into the Conduct of Local Authority Business* (Widdicombe), cmnd. 9797, HMSO, 1986.
3. *Ibid*, p. 208.
4. *Ibid*.
5. *Your Local Ombudsman,* Commission for Local Administration and the Central Office of Information, 1979; p. 1.
6. Commission for Local Administration (England), *Annual Report 1988-9,* 1989; p. 3.
8. *Ibid,* p. 29. Report by Mrs P. A. Thomas, Local Ombudsman with responsibility for the North and North Midlands.
9. *Ibid,* p. 33.
10. *Ibid,* p. 5.
11. The Representative Body is designated by the Secretary of State for the Environment to represent the authorities to whom the Act applies. However, the white paper *The Conduct of Local Authority Business* (cmnd. 433, 1988) proposes that this body should be abolished.
12. Commission for Local Administration, *Annual Report 1987-8, op. cit.*
13. *Ibid,* p. 13.
14. *Ibid,* p. 3.
15. The most important case of this kind is The Queen v the Local Ombudsman ex parte Eastleigh Borough Council, March 1988.

Chapter 13
Local Complaints
1. LGTB, *Getting Closer to the Public,* 1987. See also, for an earlier contribution, *Complaints Procedures: A Code of Practice for Local Government and Water Authorities,* The Representative Body, 1978.
2. BASW, *Clients are Fellow Citizens,* 1980.
3. National Council for Voluntary Organisations, *Clients' Rights: Report from a Working Party,* 1984.
4. The National Consumer Council (NCC) and the National Institute for Social Work (NISW), *Open to Complaints: Guidelines for Social Services Complaints Procedures,* 1988.
5. AMA and NISW, *Whose Social Services? Creating Effective Complaints Procedures in Social Service Departments,* 1988.
6. NCC, *Complaints Procedures in Social Services Departments: A Survey Report,* 1986.
7. N. Lewis, M. Seneviratne and S. Cracknell, *Complaints Procedures in Local Government,* vol. 1, Centre for Criminological and Socio-Legal Studies, University of Sheffield, nd.
8. *Ibid,* p. 122.
9. *Residential Care: A Positive Choice, op. cit.,* p. 32.
10. NCC/NISW, *Open to Complaints, op. cit.,* pp. 7-8.
11. *Caring for People, op. cit.*
12. NCC/NISW, *Open to Complaints, op. cit.,* p. 35.